Alan Pro

Dec. 26   1970

DEEP DOWN
Great Achievements in Pot-holing

Also by Garry Hogg

The 'Explorer' Books
The 'Jonty' Books
In the Nick of Time
Dangerous Trades
The Young Traveller in Norway
Country Crafts and Craftsmen

Garry Hogg

DEEP DOWN

Great Achievements in Pot-holing

HUTCHINSON OF LONDON

HUTCHINSON & CO. (*Publishers*) LTD
178–202 Great Portland Street, London, W.1

London Melbourne Sydney
Auckland Bombay Toronto
Johannesburg New York

First published 1961

*This book has been set in Baskerville type face. It has
been printed in Great Britain by The Anchor Press,
Ltd., in Tiptree, Essex, on Antique Wove paper and
bound by Taylor Garnett Evans & Co., Ltd., in
Watford, Herts*

CONTENTS

ILLUSTRATIONS

BETWEEN PAGES 60 AND 61

Entrance to the Gouffre Pierre Saint Martin

Descent of a Yorkshire pot-hole

Main Stream Passage, Peak Cavern, Castleton

Frieze of deer fording a river, Lascaux Cave

Subterranean river in the Cavern of Montespan

Ice cavern in the Eisriesenwelt

FOREWORD

THAT there exists a world beneath our own world—a 'wilderness under the earth', as it has been called—has been known to Man almost since the dawn of time. Twenty, thirty, forty thousand years ago, and more, prehistoric Man had discovered this world and claimed it for himself as a refuge from the bitter cold and from the savage animals with which he had to share the land.

It is a world of caves and passages and shafts, sub-terranean water-courses, cataracts and pits, stalagmites and stalactites, weird rock formations, great sheets and walls of eternal ice. In the course of thousands of years, when the last of the great Ice Ages had come to an end, Man finally emerged from the caverns and made his home on the surface of the earth. But this world beneath our world remained. Its secrets were lost, and in fact it is only in the last century or so that they have been rediscovered and laid bare. The men who have done this are known as speleologists; the popular word is 'caver', or 'pot-holer', and the great cave-systems they have opened up are loosely known as pot-holes.

These exist everywhere in the world where there is limestone—and that means almost universally. In Britain,

cave-systems are to be found in the Mendips: Wookey
Hole, for instance; they exist in even greater numbers in
the limestone mass of the Pennines: in Durham, the
West Riding of Yorkshire, north Derbyshire. In the south
and south-west of France most of Europe's deepest pot-
holes are to be found. There, only a few years ago, a small
party of experts reached a depth of no less than 2,959 feet
below the surface, in a pot-hole named the Gouffre Berger,
the Shepherd's Well. To date, this is the deepest pot-hole
known; but so active are pot-holers that it may well be
that by the time you read these words some even more
fantastic depth may have been plumbed and its mysteries
laid bare. Perhaps in Italy, this time, in the French-
Italian Maritime Alps, where it is believed that there is a
cave-system that may attain over 4,000 feet in depth.
Already it bears a mixed Italian-French name: Gouffre
Gaché-Piaggia Bella; and already plans are afoot to
conquer it.

Austria has limestone too, and within quite a small
radius of Salzburg there exists an extraordinary group of
caves; among them the notorious Tantalhöhle, reputedly
the most difficult—though not the deepest—pot-hole in
Europe. Here too is the Scherkofen, which has been
penetrated to a distance of 2,500 feet, beyond which no
party of cavers has ever succeeded in penetrating, though
they have not yet given up all hope.

In Germany there is a region, in the Franconian Alps,
known as 'The Land of the Thousand Caves', for no
fewer than 1,024 have already been discovered and
explored. Over the frontier, in Switzerland, there are
cave-systems such as the famous Holloch. Here some
thirty miles of tunnels, shafts, caverns, 'crawls' and

'squeezes' make up a labyrinth deep down under. It was in this cave that, only a few years ago, a party of four highly experienced pot-holers were trapped by suddenly rising water and cut off from all communication with the surface for no less than 224 hours before the flood-water subsided sufficiently for them to make their escape.

Italy, Belgium, Jugoslavia, India, China, America, Russia, New Zealand—even, surprisingly, Holland: all these countries and continents possess cave-systems and pot-holes entered with varying degrees of difficulty. Some of them have now been fully explored, surveyed and charted. Some of them are no more than points on a large-scale map, awaiting exploration. Some of them have been penetrated, have caused injury and even death among the members of the parties striving to solve their ultimate mysteries, and still retain a secret or two that may or may not be laid bare.

Pot-holing, or caving, demands courage, stamina, endurance, patience and team-spirit. It exacts the maximum from those who practise it. A pot-holer must expect to have to squeeze his body through crawls, climb up or down shafts in which ice-cold water is continuously flowing, survive temperatures below freezing-point for long periods and with no means of keeping himself warm except strenuous movement—and even this may not always be possible owing to the conditions in which he pursues his craft; he must possess a keen sense of direction; he must be level-headed, not given to panic when it seems that danger has become acute; he must be willing to take precautions and unwilling at all times to take unnecessary risks; he must be able to give orders, if he is a leader, and to accept orders unquestioningly if he is a member of a team under a leader. He has much in common with the mountaineer.

It was a famous mountaineer who, when he was asked why he expended so much effort, endured such hardship, to reach the summit of a mountain, replied briefly: 'Because it is there'. The pot-holer, if asked why he endured such discomfort and hardship, would give a similar reply.

ONE: TRAGEDY IN PEAK CAVERN

ONE fine day in October 1959 a young man took a day off from his work as a printer in Derby and boarded a train for London. He had been summoned to attend a Royal Investiture about to be held by the Duke of Edinburgh at Buckingham Palace.

In the great gathering of other people also summoned to the Investiture Ron Peters was hardly noticed, for he was so small. He stood, in fact, barely five foot high, and weighed only just seven stone—a good deal less than half the weight, for instance, of Richard Dimbleby, who happened to have been summoned to the same Investiture. Strangely enough, though, it was Ron Peters's very smallness that had enabled him, six months before, to perform the astonishing feat which now resulted in his receiving at the Duke of Edinburgh's hands the coveted George Medal.

*   *   *   *   *

Peak Cavern, only a stone's throw from the north Derbyshire village of Castleton, is one of the best-known of all our pot-hole systems. Thousands of motorists, cyclists and hikers and others come to it every year. Some are content to marvel at its imposing entrance; others stay long enough to explore its well-illuminated interior: that is to say, they wander about in the few hundred yards of cavern and corridor that are open to the general public.

But beyond that, running for two miles and more into the heart of the limestone, there extends a cave-and-shaft-and-tunnel system complex and dangerous enough to tax the skill of the most expert pot-holers in all Europe. Peak Cavern is not a place for the mere lover of adventure; its inner mysteries can be laid bare only by the experienced pot-holer, the veteran of many descents, who will treat it with the respect it deserves. It may well be that its ultimate secrets will never be revealed, so difficult of access are its remoter depths, so impossible the tortuosities of its water-worn limestone gullies and channels, steps and shafts and holes.

It was on a Sunday in March that a party of seven pot-holers, six of them members of the Sheffield branch of the British Speleological (or Pot-holing) Association, assembled at Peak Cavern, Castleton, with a specific object in view: to penetrate as far as possible a passage whose entrance had only quite recently been discovered. It was believed that it might run for a very long way into the rock and so perhaps open up a new cave system deep down.

It is hardly surprising that even the entrance to this suspected passage had only just been discovered, for it had been located some distance in from the part of Peak Cavern that was known to most visitors. The approach to it was both difficult and arduous. First, a series of chambers and passages of varying size and slope had had to be negotiated by each member of the party of seven in turn. Part of the time they were working their way downhill, part of the way uphill. Though there were no deep vertical shafts, there had been plenty of 'squeezes' and 'crawls', which had tested their ability, patience and tempers. The final 600 yards of the approach had involved belly-crawling over a thick, cold, viscous brown mud of the consistency of engineers' grease. This had clogged their clothes, worked its way up their sleeves, down their necks and into their boots and caked their hair. Though it did serve its purpose as a lubricant, facilitating movement through the tighter squeezes, it was unpleasant stuff to have to fight one's way over for 600 tedious, wriggling yards of crawl!

One by one the members of the party emerged from the tunnel and stood up and began the hopeless task of cleaning off the worst of the brown mud that clung to them. They were standing, now, in a chamber that measured about twenty feet by ten feet and ten feet high. Its floor of rock sloped steeply downwards, and as it too had a thick layer of the brown vaseline-like mud on it it was not too easy to keep one's balance. Still, even to be able to stand upright and stretch one's cramped arms and legs, after that interminable belly-crawl, was a welcome change.

The entrance to the as yet unexplored passage was located at the further end of this chamber. It consisted of a letter-box-like slit about thirty inches wide and rather less than eighteen inches high. This cavity slanted downwards at a steepish angle. The light of a pot-holer's lamp held close to it revealed only a short length, for almost immediately the tunnel began to spiral in a corkscrew fashion and so vanished from the range of the lamp. Its very shape made it a challenge to be taken up. And it was a pot-holer named Neil Moss, a twenty-year-old student who had already proved himself to be expert beyond his years, who took it up.

Because of the twisting character of the shaft, it had been agreed that no lifeline should be used for this descent: it would serve no useful purpose since, in so confined a space, there is practically no risk of falling, and the line would therefore merely be an encumbrance. Instead, a seventy-five-foot electron ladder was introduced into the shaft, its free end to be worked downwards as the pot-holer descended.

Moss entered the cavity feet foremost, his face to the rock and his arms bent in order to take as much weight as possible off his chest and stomach. He was soon well on his way, gravity helping him in his descent. Every yard or so he had to kick the ladder free where it had snagged or lodged on some projection. His aim was to keep as much of it as possible below his feet all the time; the upper end, of course, was anchored and watched over by his fellow pot-holers at the entrance to the shaft, one of whom followed him part way down so as to keep in touch with him as long as possible.

He passed with some difficulty through a bottleneck, after which he found himself in a recess which allowed him a little ease of movement. Some way below this, he found his further descent blocked by a boulder-jam that appeared to fill the shaft, and he duly reported this back to his companions, adding that he believed he might be able to kick the boulders and free the jam. This he proceeded to do. And in doing this he unwittingly took the step which was ultimately to lead to tragedy in Peak Cavern.

In loosening the jam he unfortunately caused the lower end of the electron ladder to become trapped by a boulder lower down. He did not know this, at first. What he did soon realize, however, was that the efforts he had made to free the jam had had the effect of wedging him more tightly in the tapering shaft he was attempting to descend. Those on duty at the head of the shaft found after a while that his answers to their inquiries as to progress were becoming less and less optimistic. And what is more, the sound of his voice worried them. They could hear heavy and laboured breathing, and when he did speak, his replies were brief and jerky.

Being expert pot-holers themselves, they could easily visualize the position in which their companion was now placed. He was far down a corkscrew shaft that tapered with every yard descended. Unable to reach the boulders with his hands, he was obliged to work with his feet, though unable to see exactly what he was doing. And at such a depth, and in such a constricted space, there was the constant risk of the air becoming foul with an accumulation of the deadly CO_2. Furthermore, Moss was using an acetylene lamp, which would be making a steady drain on the restricted amount of oxygen already available to him. This oxygen shortage, they rightly guessed, was the explanation of his heavy breathing and his slow and hesitant manner of replying to them. It is a basic rule among cavers to keep in touch with one another all the time. But Moss was some forty feet below them, out of sight, of course, and steadily losing contact even by word of mouth. It was developing into a grave situation.

Suddenly their anxiety was relieved. Moss called up to them to say that he thought the best thing was for him to return to the head of the shaft and let someone else have a try while he regained his strength, which, he admitted, was being sorely tried. It seemed to them an excellent suggestion and they encouraged him to make the ascent at once: he had, they assured him, done quite enough already! Then they sat back, and waited.

They waited a long time. Though they could hear sounds of laboured breathing and violent effort, there was no sign of Moss at all. They called to him, but at first there was no reply whatsoever. They called more urgently. And at last the reply came; and it was one that dashed their hopes. Moss explained, in brief sentences, that he was so tightly wedged that he could not bend a knee sufficiently to raise his foot on to a ladder rung; nor could he get toe-hold on the side of the shaft by which he could lever himself upwards against the sheer pull of gravity coupled with the friction of the rock against his clothing. In brief, he was now well and truly jammed.

His companions at the head of the shaft took swift counsel. John Randles, the leader of the expedition, made a prompt decision. Since Moss could not climb, he must be instructed to hang on to the electron ladder, and they would then haul it up the shaft with him clinging to it. It was a practical suggestion, and might have worked in spite of the corkscrew formation of the shaft—but for the fact that its lower end was immovably trapped in a boulder-jam. A preliminary haul on the ladder showed that there was enough slack for Moss to be dragged perhaps a yard up the shaft; and then it was held fast. They may have momentarily entertained the notion that they could haul on it strongly enough to break off the lower end where it was gripped; but it was not a notion that promised well. It was in fact just as likely that if the ladder broke at all it would do so above, instead of below, the trapped pot-holer. And in any case the breaking-strain on a good electron ladder is so high that there was little likelihood that it would break at all.

The alternative suggestion, now, was to lower a rope down the shaft. This was quickly done, and Moss was told to make himself fast to it and give them the word to haul away. It would be an uncomfortable passage, in a shaft so twisted, but it now seemed the only solution. They listened for his signal to haul. It was a very long time in coming. When he did call up to them it was to report that in spite of the most violent efforts he had found it impossible to get the rope round him. He had managed to reach out and grip the end of the rope, but he had not the elbow-room to wrap it round himself.

They called out to him to let go and stand by; they would think again. Next time the rope was lowered it had a loop on it, large enough to pass over his head and shoulders. Moss grasped it, and after a series of almost superhuman efforts, contrived to slip it first over one shoulder and then over the other, so that it could be anchored beneath his armpits. He signalled that he was ready, and the men at the head of the shaft took the strain. They increased their weight on it carefully, well aware that five men hauling on a rope that was wrapped round one man's ribs would inevitably produce almost unbearable pressure on them. Nevertheless, there was no alternative solution.

The rope began to move. Only inches at first; then a

foot; then another foot and yet another foot—perhaps a yard and more. Then movement ceased. They lay back on the rope again, increasing their weight; but still the rope remained immovable. They could guess what had happened: after being hauled a yard or so up the shaft, Moss had been caught in a constriction and gripped by its rough walls. They tried again, first calling down to him to be ready for what might be a very bad moment or two. And then the worst happened: the rope broke. The five men were thrown backwards to the ground, and Moss dropped back to the point in the shaft from which he had only just been hauled. It was not entirely surprising: though the rope was of first-class quality, and had been checked all along its length for any possible flaw, it had had to take an immense strain—and at the same time pass over a series of rock projections, some smooth, some jagged; inevitably its strands had been badly frayed, and had eventually broken.

In spite of his appalling predicament, Moss remained astonishingly cheerful. The rope, he reported, had broken off not far above his head. He now had the lower end in his hands. If they would lower a new rope he would make it fast to the short end that was still attached to him, and they could have another try. They did so; and again the rope broke. When they hauled it up and inspected it they could see at once the damage that had been done to it as it took the strain in that corkscrew shaft with its jagged rock projections.

The situation now looked grim indeed. The electron ladder was jammed; and they now realized that even if it could have been freed there was only a very small chance that it could be hauled up a shaft of this nature. If a rope snagged and broke, how much more likely were the metal rungs of a ladder to be snagged on the same jutting fragments of rock, and held fast. What had been, until then, a comparatively minor operation had now swelled to one of major proportions. If Moss was to be extracted from this diabolical corkscrew shaft, then assistance was needed—and it must come soon.

Two members of the party therefore set off as fast as they could go to cover the two miles underground back to the entrance to Peak Cavern to give the alarm and recruit expert and professional help. The others remained behind, to keep in touch with their companion and encourage him as best they could. By this time they themselves were exhausted from their efforts at hauling on the rope in cramped circumstances; they were cold and wet and hungry, and becoming more and more anxious as the minutes dragged by and they seemed no nearer to rescuing their young companion.

They took it in turns to maintain contact with him by descending a little way down the shaft and talking to him. But even this was not an entirely good thing. For by wedging himself in the upper end of the shaft, a man was preventing the circulation of what little air there was lower down. And as each man returned to the top of the shaft he reported that it seemed to him that the air in the shaft was becoming progressively more and more foul.

It was undoubtedly the steadily mounting accumulation of foul air that accounted for the deterioration in Moss's speech when they called out to him. Whereas to begin with he had been clear-headed and co-operative, now his replies had become vague and irrelevant to the situation.

His mind seemed to be 'wandering'. And after a while there were no further replies from him to anything.

At first this frightened those who were watching at the head of the shaft: it seemed that he must have died. On the other hand, one of them pointed out, it was more likely that he had merely fallen unconscious. And this, surprising as it may seem, could be an advantage. For when a man falls unconscious his rate of breathing drops substantially; and the quantity of air he takes in drops substantially too. This could mean, they told themselves, that Moss might survive longer, unconscious, than he would if he were breathing fast and deeply, as he would do if he were making a continuous effort to free himself.

It was the only hopeful element—if it could truly be called that—in the whole desperate situation. Meanwhile, all they could do was to remain on the alert, listening for any sounds from below, in the darkness of the shaft, and counting the minutes, almost the seconds, until they heard the advance-guard of the newly recruited rescue-party approaching. Every minute seemed to them a long-drawn-out hour of anxiety.

Among the first to turn up was the highly experienced R.A.F. Mountain Rescue Unit from Harpur Hill, Derbyshire, alerted by their very efficient Tannoy alarm system. A rescue team consisting of tough, experienced miners came post-haste from Chesterfield, despatched by the National Coal Board. Pot-holers and pot-hole rescue units came in from far and near to offer their services individually and collectively. From hospitals and other sources of supply came oxygen cylinders and pumps and rubber pipe-lines. The police, ambulance outfits, fire-brigade men, Civil Defence workers from a dozen centres, converged on the little Derbyshire township of Castleton. A Royal Navy submarine rescue squad answered the general S O S sent out by the police. The G.P.O. sent a complete field-telephone outfit, together with engineers to install and operate it, so that the workers two miles inside Peak Cavern could keep in direct touch with the outside world and summon whatever additional assistance they might need with the least possible delay.

All in all, there must eventually have been no fewer than 300 people engaged on the rescue operation. Of these, something like 200 were themselves experienced pot-holers, summoned to the scene by telephone and telegram and S O S messages broadcast by the B.B.C. Such an army of helpers entailed elaborate feeding arrangements, and the local W.V.S. set up a base at which sandwiches and hot drinks could be obtained at any hour of the day or night. The people of Castleton and the neighbourhood threw open their cottages so that any worker coming off duty from a shift underground could get a bath and a change of clothing and somewhere to rest before starting work again.

John Randles had reported that the further end of the shaft was so constricted that only a slimly built man could hope to penetrate it beyond a certain point. It was, he told the men who came through to the underground chamber which was the main base of the rescue operation, so difficult a series of corkscrews and spirals, with jagged edges waiting to trap and cut the ropes, that every movement would have to be made with the utmost caution; to hurry would mean to double the risk of disaster.

There was room in the cavern which lay at the further end of the 600-yard belly-crawl through the brown

clinging mud for only twenty or thirty men at most at any
one time. This was the operational base. To it, by way
of the sludge-filled tunnel, all the tackle had to be
manœuvred: the oxygen cylinders, the air-pumps, the
lighting equipment, the ropes, rope-ladders, grapnels,
the crowbars, the vacuum-flasks containing hot drinks
for those working at the 'face', the food-concentrates,
the first-aid boxes. A highly organized routine kept a
succession of men crawling through from one end to the
other, and a shift system was developed so that there
were always men present at operational base who were
reasonably fresh and fit while others rested and recouped
their energies in order to be able to take their place when
the time came. No one was foolish enough to imagine that
this rescue was going to be either simple or swift. Nevertheless, everyone knew that time was all-important: a pot-
holer was wedged, unconscious, in a narrow shaft, with
foul air all about him.

The first member of any rescue unit to make an attempt
to reach him was the M.O. from the R.A.F. Mountain
Rescue Unit, Flt-Lieut. Carter. He very quickly established that there was carbonic acid gas in the shaft, and he
knew very well that there is only a relatively limited time
during which anyone can breathe in this. He came to it
first at twenty feet; at twenty-five feet it was bad enough
to frighten him. He himself only managed to keep going
by inhaling oxygen piped down to him by his assistants
stationed at the entrance to the shaft.

Incredible as it must seem, Carter remained for no less
than twelve hours in the shaft, maintaining the flow of
oxygen and keeping it in circulation as best he could in
the ten or fifteen feet that separated him from the uncon-

scious pot-holer. He was so cramped that every slightest movement he made demanded a great muscular effort and a concentration of sheer will-power. When, at the end of his twelve-hour spell, he was finally persuaded to return, he had barely the strength to work his way up the twenty-five feet or so to the exit.

His place was immediately taken by a civilian doctor from Buxton. By that time it was early afternoon on the day following Moss's entry into the shaft. Twenty hours had gone by since Moss had last spoken; yet the doctor was able to confirm Flt-Lieut. Carter's statement that he was still breathing. Though his breathing was laboured and irregular, it was audible; while he breathed, he was alive; there was hope, the rescuers believed.

Hope of rescue, however, was now known to depend on one thing: the arrival of a pot-holer of experience who was small, strong and lithe enough to be able not only to reach Neil Moss but to bend down and fasten some sort of harness round him by which he could be hauled bodily out of the shaft. This rescuer would have to work his way back up the shaft, feeding the ropes past all those dangerous rock projections, or the rescue attempt would fail like the first.

An S O S went out for lightweight pot-holers. Two men, much smaller, more slightly built, than those who had already tried and failed, entered the cavern, fought their way through the tunnel to the operational base in the chamber and asked to be allowed to make the attempt to reach Moss at the end of the forty-foot shaft. First one of them, and then the other, however, in spite of their determination, in spite of the oxygen pumped down to them, blacked-out and had to be withdrawn on their own ropes and revived by artificial respiration. It was not their fault; there had been a breakdown in the pipe-line which was not immediately detected. But they had shown that they were still too heavily built to go far down the shaft.

Then a third pot-holer appeared. He had squirmed his way faster than most through the long, sludge-filled tunnel, and arrived in the chamber among the operational base workers like a cork exploding out of a bottle. He was by far the smallest man to have appeared until that moment. If he stood five foot even in his boots, it would be surprising. He was so slightly built that even in his mud-caked pot-holer's rig he looked like a child. But it was obvious from his handshake, from the way he moved, that he was wiry, close-knit, lithe and strong. He introduced himself as Ron Peters.

He wasted no time. He picked the length of rope he fancied—light but strong, like himself, coiled it expertly about his shoulders so that it would be easy to uncoil when the time came, and, having been fitted with a mouthpiece attached to the oxygen supply, nodded briefly, and entered the letter-box opening to the shaft with a neat, quick movement; in a matter of seconds the lamp attached to his helmet had vanished round the first twist of the spiral shaft. Those on duty at the operational base looked at one another; tired and anxious as they were after their long vigil, they felt real hope at last.

Ron Peters moved fast. Ten, twenty, thirty, thirty-five feet of rope ran out through the hands of those standing by. Forty feet. He actually succeeded in touching with one foot the helmet of the trapped pot-holer he had come to rescue. By some miraculous feat of contortion, worthy of an acrobat, he contrived to bend down and attach his

rope to the loose end of the broken rope worn by Moss.
But by then, in spite of the oxygen, he was almost literally
at his last gasp. He signalled for help in getting out, and
began to work his way upwards, helped by the tension on
his own rope.

Partway to the exit, however, he found breathing easier,
and checked his upward movement. Deliberately he
wedged himself in the shaft at a point where he would be
able to check the passage of Moss's rope as it ran close to
the projections of rock that had cut through the rope the
previous day. He signalled to those at the top to haul
away. In the light of his lamp he saw the rope strain and
quiver as they heaved on it. It moved a foot, perhaps
eighteen inches, upwards. Then, taut as a bow-string, it
quivered, but moved no further. And then, suddenly—it,
too, broke!

Ron Peters followed the loose end up the shaft and
gathered himself together for a second attempt. It was
obvious that Neil Moss must be wedged very tightly
indeed, for the breaking-strain on the rope was high and
the two men hauling on it ought to have been able to
shift him, between them.

It was John Randles who noticed a disquieting feature
of this second rescue attempt: the rope that had broken
had been the rope that was round Neil Moss's body. If he
was to be extricated from the shaft, a rope would have to
be not merely attached to his harness, but looped round
him. This would involve an almost impossible feat of
acrobatism.

'I'll have another bash!' Ron Peters said, briefly. 'Give
me plenty of spare rope; and make sure the oxygen's
okay. The gas is pretty bad down there.'

He entered the shaft again. Those on the rope watched him as he vanished once more round the first twist of the spiral. Ten, twenty, thirty, thirty-five feet of rope once more ran out through the hands of his supporters. They held it carefully, concentrating on the feel of it. Since he had an oxygen mouthpiece on, any signals he sent up would have to be rope signals. Meanwhile, Ron Peters struggled at the base of the shaft to get his hands low enough to place a noose round the shoulders of the trapped pot-holer. In the silence down there he could hear breathing. Was it just his own, or not? He held his breath. No, it was Moss, after all: he was alive yet!

But for all his frantic efforts to get the rope round him, he was unable to do so. He used up all but a fraction of his strength in the desperate struggle, but eventually had to give up. With just enough strength in his arms and legs to complete the return journey, he fought his way back, slithered out into the cavern, and admitted defeat.

'But he's *still* breathing?' someone asked him, incredulously. 'After all these hours?'

Ron Peters nodded. He was too exhausted, too defeated, to find words. He would never have believed that he would be beaten by it.

'If he is still breathing, he's just *got* to be fetched out!' John Randles announced. 'There *must* be a way, somehow.'

'Could I have a shot?'

A newcomer had appeared among them. About as unexpected as anyone could be, down there. Not a man, this time, but—a girl! She stood before the members of the operational base, smeared from head to foot in the viscous brown mud through which she had just finished belly-crawling, blinking in the strong lamplight. 'I'm smaller than Ron Peters,' she said. 'And I'm fairly tough.'

June Bailey was eighteen years old, well under five feet tall, and very slim. She had been an enthusiastic pot-holer ever since she had first persuaded her parents to let her take up the hobby. It had been hard work persuading them to let her join in the rescue work, but she had managed it at last, and had just arrived from her Manchester home. John Randles was not happy about letting her try: she was younger than the other would-be rescuers, and he did not know how experienced she really was. Still, a life was at stake; there was always just a chance. . . .

She roped up, fitted her oxygen mask and was lowered into the shaft. Once more the rope ran out: twenty, thirty, almost forty feet this time. By twisting her neck round till she could have cried with pain, she managed to see how it was that he was so firmly jammed. One arm was locked across a bottleneck in the shaft which at widest was hardly wider than his body. The result was that the harder the rope was tugged at, the more firmly the arm was jammed into the cavity.

She did not wait to find out whether he was breathing still, but came back up the shaft as fast as she could move, the rough projections of rock ripping at the tough material of which her overalls were made.

'You'll have to let me down *head first*, this time,' she announced, breathlessly. 'Then I can free his arm and put the harness round him so that it will pull him clear.' Her voice trembled with eagerness. She turned to the leader of the party. 'You must!' she insisted. 'It's our only hope!'

'Forty feet down a shaft that width, and *head first*!' John

C

Randles shook his head. There was no doubt whatsoever in his mind that that would mean a double tragedy. 'Sorry, June.' He was adamant.

What she had not realized was something in fact quite simple. To work her way *down* a forty-foot shaft would not be impossible; not even really difficult. But when the time came to return she would have to work her way *up* the shaft, feet foremost; and this, in a spiral shaft, even with the help of a rope, would be impossible. It would not even be possible to rescue her from above, either.

Bitterly disappointed, but accepting his decision, June Bailey made a second descent, feet foremost. But again she had to return to the top of the shaft and, like Ron Peters, admit defeat. She was helped out through the long tunnel and the chamber beyond, out to the fresh air beyond the entrance to Peak Cavern, and there taken charge of by the medical staff on duty.

At midday on the following day, just forty-eight hours after he had first lowered himself into the mouth of the unexplored tunnel two miles from the entrance, Neil Moss died. Flt-Lieut. Carter, who had been the first to attempt a rescue with the use of oxygen, and who had taken turn and turn about with Dr Eccles, of Buxton, in keeping a flow of oxygen in the shaft, came up with the news that he could no longer detect any sign of breathing at all. So far as they knew, the unhappy pot-holder had died of gas poisoning without ever regaining consciousness. The wonder was that he had survived as long as he had.

Easter was at hand. Normally thousands of people come to Peak Cavern over that holiday week-end; in 1959 its entrance was closed to visitors and police remained on duty day and night. There were always the morbid-minded who might want to have a look at the setting for the drama that had now ended.

After Easter, elaborate plans were made for the recovery of the body. There were some people who felt it would be better to seal off the shaft; others, however, felt that there might be some way of entering it from the side. Rock-drilling tackle was assembled, with experts to handle it; a number of experienced pot-holers stood by. It was established that a thirty-foot-thick limestone mass lay between the men with the drills and the point at which it was believed Neil Moss's body was jammed.

Rock-drilling is an arduous job at best; the drillers here had to work in conditions which made it almost impossible for them to control their apparatus. Attempt after attempt was made; each attempt in turn was defeated by the sheer mass of hard limestone. Drills broke, supply-lines failed, rubble piled up and had to be negotiated if the hole was to be made any deeper. In the end the experts had to admit that they were defeated. They dismantled their gear and carried it laboriously away through the constricted tunnels and chambers that lay between them and the entrance. The alternative had to be accepted.

The letter-box entrance to the unexplored shaft, down which first John Randles and Peter Sandall, then Flt-Lieut. Carter, then Ron Peters and lastly June Bailey, had striven to rescue Neil Moss, was sealed off with stones and rubble. Operation Rescue—one of the most elaborate and strenuously maintained in all pot-holing history—had failed; the ultimate secret of Peak Cavern remained, and still remains, a secret.

TWO: LONE VENTURE

'IN HIGH SUMMER, monsieur,' the peasant said, 'it might just be possible. If the weather has long been very dry, then only a little water flows out of the mountainside. A strong and determined man might wade against its stream.'

Two boys, sons of the mountain peasant, strong and tough-looking, came across to see what the stranger was talking about with their father. What, they wondered, was he after?

'These two boys,' the peasant went on, 'being young and foolish, thought they could penetrate the mountainside in spite of the force of the water. They believed there was buried treasure to be found. The younger one was overwhelmed by the water and his elder brother only just saved him. It was touch and go, believe me, monsieur.' He turned to the boys. 'Is that not so, *mes enfants?*' They nodded emphatically. '*C'est tout-à-fait impossible, m'sieur!*' they assured him.

It was a word that Norbert Casteret had never admitted to his vocabulary. 'Difficult', 'dangerous', certainly: but 'impossible'? Nothing, he firmly believed, was impossible. This, then, was a challenge he must at once take up, if only to prove that his beliefs were sound.

*   *   *   *   *

It is exceptionally rare today for any pot-holer, however experienced, to pioneer a cave-system on his own. Experience has proved that there should always be a minimum of two men, and better still a team of three, four or more. In this way the leader can be sure of support, communication with the outside world can be maintained and the chances of successful exploration very greatly increased.

There have, however, been examples of lone exploration that have exceeded the wildest hopes of those who embarked upon them. One of the most outstanding is the exploration of the Cavern of Montespan, in the Pyrenees. The man who carried it through was Norbert Casteret, a Frenchman, one of the greatest speleologists of all time. The limestone of the Hautes Pyrenees and Haute Garonne, in the south-west corner of France, has always been his best pot-holing territory.

His conversation with the peasant on the Pyrenean hillside near Montespan took place in his earlier days, before he had become the veteran he is today. He was in the stage of evolving techniques and trying them out for himself. The Cavern of Montespan was the setting for one of the boldest of his experiments: an experiment that only a man of immense courage and self-confidence as well as innate skill would have dared to undertake.

A day or two after his conversation with the peasant he climbed the mountainside, alone, till he came to the opening he was after. It was about the size of a man's body bent double, and it was almost completely filled with a stream of water flowing out strongly through it and then down the mountainside.

Casteret stripped to a pair of trunks, folded his clothes

into a pile and then boldly thrust himself, like a cork into a bottleneck, into the aperture. So great was the force of water flowing from it that he had to claw at the sides to prevent himself from being swept clean out of it in a backwards somersault. But he succeeded in entering. And once inside, found himself, as he had anticipated, in a cavern, or a wide tunnel, perhaps ten feet across and high. Because it was not so constricted, the stream of water was wider and shallower, and flowed with much less strength. He had gambled on this, and the gamble had paid off.

Beneath his feet there was rock, with a covering of sand. Wading in the stream, he worked his way forward for about fifty yards, at which point the tunnel bent sharply to the right. At the same time the tunnel roof dipped steeply; after a few yards it had come so low that Casteret was obliged to bend almost double in order to make any headway. For twenty or thirty yards he continued in this cramped position, his face only just clear of the water. Then the tunnel roof dipped again, this time so steeply that it came down below the surface of the water. His way, apparently, was now blocked.

The obvious thing to do was to turn back. But Casteret had never liked turning back. He stood there, bent low beneath the roof, his chin in the cold water of the underground stream, and thought hard. This tunnel, or long, narrow cave, interested him deeply. Unlike most of the pot-holes he had hitherto penetrated, this one was mainly horizontal. He had a shrewd idea that, this being the case, it might well have been used by Man in remote prehistoric times, and he wanted to check his theory for himself. Other underground passages like this one had produced valuable information of the kind always being sought for by archaeologists. This one might do so, too!

'I'll go on!' he announced to himself, in the dark, cold, watery tunnel; there was no one else to speak to.

In making this decision Casteret was showing a sheer cool courage that would be hard to match in any sphere of human activity. If he was to go on, he would have to duck down beneath the surface of the water and part-swim, part-wade, in complete darkness—into the unknown. He would have to fill his lungs with sufficient air to see him through to a point at which the tunnel roof rose again, so that he could refill them from the pocket of air he would find. If there was no such pocket of air awaiting him, then he might try to return before he used up his last gasp of air. If he failed, then he would drown. If he succeeded, then he was merely back once again at his starting-point, no better off than before. It was an appalling risk that he was taking.

There was a narrow ledge of rock alongside him, just clear of the water. He melted a little wax, made a puddle of it, and stood a lighted candle in it before the wax hardened. It would stand there: a miniature lighthouse to mark his starting-point, a tiny yellow flame in the vast empty darkness all about him. If he had to swim back, it would be the beacon he would make for.

Without wasting any more time, Casteret began a series of deep breaths, each deeper than the last. Being an extremely practical man, fond of human experimenting, he knew exactly how long he could hold his breath in varying conditions: between two and three minutes if he was relaxed; a few seconds over two minutes if he was swimming. It was self-knowledge well worth having.

Immediately he had filled his lungs for the third time he ducked beneath the water. Partly swimming, partly pushing himself forward with one foot, his hands outstretched like giant antennae to keep in contact with the rock wall on either side and at the same time to protect himself against any unsuspected projection, he worked his way forward, holding his breath determinedly. All the time he pressed forward he had to bear in mind that there existed a 'point of no return'. If he moved forward for more than a minute, he had breath for just one minute left to him. If he turned at that point, he could regain safety; if he went on, then he must find air within sixty seconds, no more. If he failed—it would be the end for him.

Fortune, they say (but it is a dangerous theory to work on!), favours the brave. At the end of the second minute he found that the roof had receded a little. He lifted his head almost clear of the water: he had come to a pocket of air! He emptied his lungs of the last gasp of air he had been retaining, and breathed the cool air deeply, once, twice, and again. He was filled with a tremendous sense of elation. He had performed for the first time one of the most difficult and dangerous feats that any pot-holer ever has to attempt: it is technically known as 'forcing a siphon'. Norbert Casteret is almost certainly the first man ever known to have performed the feat, though others have achieved it since, under his inspiration.

Having refilled his lungs, he turned round and swam back to his starting-point. The candle was burning quietly in the still air. He snatched it up, impatient now to get out of the tunnel: not to be done with the whole enterprise but to make more elaborate preparations for a second, and deeper, investigation. He left the tunnel, slipped out through the aperture in the side of the mountain, put on his clothes, and returned for the night to Montespan. And he said nothing to anyone there about what he had done, or intended to do.

Next day, still alone, he climbed the mountainside again. He had with him extra candles, matches in a watertight box, and a close-fitting bathing-cap of rubber. Once again he thrust himself through the opening, fighting the water that poured out through it. Once again he waded along the water-filled tunnel. He came to the ledge where his candle had burned, planted a new candle on it and lit it. Then he packed a number of short lengths of candle, and his tin of matches, inside his rubber cap, took his three powerful breaths and for the second time plunged into the siphon.

Casteret has always had a 'photographic' memory for rock surfaces—even, strange as it may seem, for those on which he has never set eyes. His eyes were in his finger-tips, like those of a blind man. By sense of touch alone he recognized and identified every knob and projection of rock, every hollow and cranny, in the walls and roof of the water-filled tunnel he was now passing through for the second time. He bobbed upwards exactly as the roof hollow came within reach, expelled his breath and again breathed deeply in, filling his lungs.

Then, with infinite caution, he extracted a stub of candle and lit it with one of his precious matches. He peered into the darkness ahead. For a yard or two, any-way, he could see there was a space between the surface of the water and the tunnel roof. Good enough! He worked his way forward again, his chin barely clear of the water.

The roof was uncomfortably close overhead, and from time to time he cracked his skull on some projection he could not see. He came to a second siphon. He breathed in deeply, and plunged for the second time into the unknown. And for the second time emerged into clean, cold air just in time. His luck was certainly holding!

Eventually he emerged into a big chamber. He lit several candles in the hope of ascertaining its dimensions, but all he could be sure of was that its roof was at least thirty feet above him. All about him there were enormous boulders, tumbled on the rock floor of the chamber and piled in crazy-looking pyramids that looked as though they might topple over at a touch. They had broken away, he guessed, from the roof. But they must be pretty firmly rooted because the stream flowed through and among them without shifting them.

He was glad to be out of the tunnel and to feel less cramped. Glad to be able to breathe freely, too. But though there was all the air he wanted, it now made breathing painful because there was a substantial drop in the temperature: the air he sucked in made his nostrils quiver with the cold. He was wearing nothing but bathing-trunks, and the cold air played over his body, bringing gooseflesh to every inch of it. He tried to warm himself by doing gymnastics, but it was difficult on a floor encumbered with rocks and wet with running water. He remembered that it had been warmer in the water of the tunnel than in this chamber, and at once went forward to find where the water was coming from.

The tunnel, he found, continued beyond the pile of boulders. To begin with it was wider than the one he had just left, but soon it began to narrow; and at the same time the roof began to descend steeply towards the surface of the water. In fact he soon found that he was working his way not so much into a tunnel as into a funnel. Certainly, however, it was warmer in the water than in the cold air of the chamber he had just left.

The roof came lower. A few yards ahead of him he could see that in fact it touched the water: he had come to yet another siphon! What he had done a couple of times, he told himself, he could, and would, do again. He put a lighted candle on a narrow rock ledge, made sure that he had candle-ends and matches hermetically sealed in his rubber cap, breathed in deeply, and plunged.

It proved to be a much more uncomfortable siphon than the others. Instead of being smooth, the roof was armed with jagged down-pointing stalactites, only a few inches in length but long and sharp enough to give him some murderous stabs as he bobbed along beneath them. The floor, too, was treacherous. At times he dropped into hollows; when he climbed up from them he jabbed his head and shoulders against the stalactites. He had to concentrate hard on merely holding his breath, or the pain of a sudden stab might have caused him to expel it in one gasp, and then he would be done for. Casteret remembered the forcing of that siphon all his long life as a pot-holer.

But his breath once more held. He emerged, cold, exhausted, dazed with pain and—for once in his life—truly frightened. He wished that he had a companion with him. There is no loneliness quite like loneliness in the dark; and when the darkness is that of deep down under it takes immense courage and fortitude not to panic.

He now found himself in another cavern, with a series

of corridors leading out of it. The floor had a thin carpet of clay on it, wet where the stream ran over it, dryish elsewhere. He welcomed the existence of the clay; and for two reasons. The first was that it helped to confirm his theory that prehistoric Man had used this underground system of caverns and passages, for it was the sort of place he was known to have favoured; the second was that he himself could leave his footprints in the clay, and follow them back if he were to lose himself in any of the corridors.

Once again, however, the cavern turned into a funnel: walls closed in, roof lowered, the quantity of water seemed to increase. Once again he had to force his way forward. But this time the walls continued to close in on him, instead of running parallel. He was reduced to thrusting himself forward in a sideways position. At length he reached a point at which he had to let out his breath, for if he breathed in fully his chest was jammed against the rock, his shoulders at the same time wedged against it: he had reached the limit of movement at last. The tunnel was now no more than a fissure in the rock: a pygmy could have gone no further.

At first Casteret was filled with despair: his theory about prehistoric occupation of the Cavern of Montespan looked as though it had been proved false. And then the strangest, most unexpected, thing happened: he found in the water in which he was standing a whole flotilla of—tadpoles! This enormously excited him. For he was enough of a naturalist to know that tadpoles need a certain amount of light, and the minute particles of life-giving vegetable-matter only to be found in water that is warmed and fed from the *outside*. He had never encountered tadpoles in the water usually found in pot-holes.

Therefore, he concluded, he must have passed right through the mountain by way of an almost level cavern-and-passage system, and must now be within yards at most of the point at which the tadpoles had entered it!

To the layman it might seem that he had in fact accomplished very little: no more than the discovery that it was possible to pass from one slope of a mountain to the other by a subterranean channel. But Casteret knew better. For he had discovered something infinitely more important than the presence of the tadpoles. In bending down to try to catch some of them for inspection he had touched something smooth, round, hard—and detached from the rock. When he shone his light on it he knew at once what it was: a bison's tooth!

This told him a great deal. He knew that no bison could possibly have penetrated this underground labyrinth; therefore, the tooth had been brought here by some *human agency*. And this must have happened thousands upon thousands of years before, because it was an immense time since bison had roamed in south-western France. Primitive Man had had to fight for living-space with these shaggy, dangerous creatures; the tooth belonged to one that he had succeeded in killing. He had brought it into this cavern system, to be shaped into a weapon or a tool, perhaps, or used for some secret purpose of his own. For here he had lived, worked, worshipped, brought up his family; and this solitary bison tooth was the clue to it all!

Autumn came, and the flow of water increased. No longer was it a series of rock pipes and siphons: the whole of the tunnel was filled. But the summer of 1923 was an exceptionally dry one, and Norbert Casteret took the first opportunity he had of returning to Montespan. He brought with him an expert pot-holing friend, Henri Godin. Together they penetrated the hole in the mountainside, delighted to find the flow of water substantially less than it had been the previous year. They found the tunnels and caverns much easier to penetrate. They found, too, that there were side galleries, smaller chambers, opening off the main tunnel, which Casteret had guessed at but never seen during his first exploration.

One of these was 650 feet long, on a slightly higher level than the others, and as a result, dry as a bone from end to end. After about 600 feet it bent sharply to one side and narrowed; the roof came lower; they had to walk in single file, their heads bent low to keep clear of the rock projections above them. Then came a stretch 100 feet long in which they had to lie flat on their stomachs and wriggle like lizards, using toes, knees and elbows. Beyond that, they emerged into a chamber in which they could stand upright at last: an enormous relief to them both.

They inspected it. There was a skimming of clay on the floor and on the walls too. In some parts the clay on the walls was quite deep. Casteret took from his belt a small trowel which he had brought with him, rather to Godin's surprise, and began picking at it. He used his tool with care, for on it a good deal depended: final confirmation of his belief, partly confirmed by the finding of the bison tooth, that in remote times Man had entered here.

Little by little, he stripped away the skin of clay that had accumulated on the lower part of the walls of the chamber as a result of the action of water carrying silt along during the flood periods. And on the walls he found, one at a time, what he had hardly dared to hope he would find: rock engravings.

He found horse and hyena, lion, bear and bison and other animals, some of them now extinct in Europe, others known in the wilder parts of Central Europe. His excitement was tremendous: he could hardly contain himself. And when, after further visits, and many long hours spent in this newly discovered subterranean chamber, he unearthed a number of hand-worked flints, and piles of flint chippings which made it clear that Man had shaped his flints inside that very cavern, his excitement knew no bounds.

But there was more still to come. He unearthed a number of hardened clay statuettes: models of bears and other wild animals in miniature, thirty in all. And among them he found some of the beautifully shaped bone spatulas which Man had used to fashion the clay to these strange likenesses. He almost believed he could discern the fingerprints of the artists who had worked with them, embedded in the soft clay.

Archaeologists were enormously impressed: it was rare indeed for anything of the kind to be discovered in such perfect condition. They flocked to the little village of Montespan to inspect Casteret and Godin's finds, examine them and catalogue them. Experts among them agreed that the finds were the work of Magdalenian Man: this meant that they were not less than 20,000 years old! They rivalled the prehistoric finds from the famous Tuc d'Audoubert, in the Ariège. Had Casteret not taken up the challenge of the peasant, had he not had the courage to force that siphon, they might be undiscovered to this day.

THREE: FLIGHT OF A MILLION BATS

'I'll go round 'em up,' Jim White said. 'You boys just take it easy!' He slipped the halter from the stockyard post and jumped into the saddle. 'See there's something left for me to eat when I get back. I'm hungry right now!'

He glanced back over his shoulder as he rode away, by no means sure that he was not a fool to have said he would do the job on his own. Hadn't he been out all day, working the ranch with his two partners, and so deserving a rest in the evening as much as they did? Still, he had offered to go; he would have to see the job through. The mystery was: how had those beasts got out, anyway? Ah well, they had got out: that was all there was to it! Or— was it?

*　　　*　　　*　　　*　　　*

The ranch that belonged to Jim White and his two partners was on the plain under the shadow of the Guadalupe Mountains, on the border dividing the State of Texas from that of New Mexico. On much of it there was cactus and prickly pear. To move fast across it, when the light was failing, was to risk being badly cut about the legs by the hard spines, that seemed to have an almost diabolical knack of extending their points when any creature on four legs or two came near, and injecting the poison. Jim White kept his eyes on the level of his horse's flanks, not liking to raise them for fear of becoming a victim.

Nevertheless, as he approached the first slopes of the Guadalupe Mountains his attention was momentarily distracted by what appeared from a distance to be a great column of smoke rising in a curious funnel-like formation from the mountainside. His quick eye noted a peculiarity about it, too: though the usual evening breeze had sprung up, this column of smoke did not appear to be in the slightest affected by it. Instead, it was rising vertically to a considerable height, and then fanning out to all points of the compass so that it looked like a huge inverted cone in the sky.

'Wall, gol-darn it!' said Jim White, and spurred his horse in the direction of what was so much puzzling him. For the time being he had entirely forgotten that he was supposed to be rounding up part of the herd.

He very soon discovered that what he had assumed to be a column of smoke was in fact a column of—bats! This grey, funnel-shaped cloud high in the air consisted of millions of bats. Millions upon millions. Having reined-in his horse, he stayed in his saddle to watch. The ascending cloud of bats seemed endless. He had been motionless there for nearly an hour before there was any sign of a thinning-out of the cloud. But in another quarter of an hour the stream had thinned to a mere trickle: that of the rearguard of the bats, now following the main body, and

D

all going in search of the insects that constituted their evening meal.

He spurred his horse and went forward again, making for the dark patch of mountainside from which the cloud had emerged. When he came to it there were still a few bats emerging from it, in clusters of a dozen or so. It was a cavity in the stony earth which he did not remember having seen before. But by now most of the evening light had drained away; the mountainside was in deep shadow. So he gathered together a bundle of dry grass, put a match to it, and tossed it over the lip of the aperture, bending over to peer down at it as it fell.

It seemed to him to fall for a surprisingly long time. It must be, he thought, a pretty deep shaft. Or perhaps a vast underground cavern. Yes, it must be that: nothing smaller would have roof and wall area sufficient for the myriad bats he had just seen coming away from it and which therefore must live down there. This, he decided, needed further probing.

A day or two later, without having in the meantime said anything to his two partners for fear of being laughed at, Jim White set off with several coils of rope, an oil-lamp and an axe. Quickly he reached the aperture in the mountainside. There he hitched the ends of two ropes to a heavy boulder, which he first tested to make sure that it would not budge if a strain was put on it. Then, carrying his axe in his belt and his lamp on a piece of cord slung over his shoulder, he lowered himself over the edge of the hole and began to descend. He had knotted his two ropes at intervals so that he would be able to climb down and up them more easily. He had no idea of course whether they would be long enough; but he relied on his muscular strength and the wiry, whipcord sinews of his frame, to get him back up the improvised ladder when the moment arrived.

After a while he felt one toe touch solid rock. He tested it, and it felt firm. Cautiously he stepped off the rope and put both feet together, still hanging on firmly with both hands. He could see nothing at all, except a spot of blue sky far above his head, as though seen through the wrong end of a telescope. All about him, and below him: just blackness. But the ledge seemed solid. He released one hand, struck a match and lit his lamp. It did not give much light, but enough to show that he was on a ledge partway down a shaft, with another ledge—or possibly the base of the shaft: he hoped so—just within view beneath him. But, more promising: there was the entrance to what looked like a tunnel, branching away from the ledge he was standing on. Jim White resolved to explore this.

He worked his way across the ledge, moving with extreme caution now that he had let go of his ropes, and found himself on the threshold of the tunnel. The faint glow of his storm lantern did little more than stir up the surrounding darkness. Still, it was a comfort to him, deep down here as he now was. And it encouraged him to move forward, small as it was. He came eventually to a great chamber with a smooth rock floor. His light was insufficient to indicate its size, but he had the impression that it was vast. He walked about on the floor, first to one side, then to the other, his lantern making a round yellow pool of light at his feet, but little more than that.

Enough, though, to save his life. For glancing down at it at one point, he found himself on the very edge of a chasm that yawned beneath him immediately in front of his feet. To estimate its depth he tossed a stone down it, listening intently for the sound of the stone hitting the bottom. The stone seemed to him to take a fearful time to reach it! Perhaps, he thought, it was time he turned round and worked his way back to his starting-point?

He had just decided to do this when, to his horror, the little yellow flame in his lantern flickered and expired! It had run out of paraffin. For a moment Jim White came near to panic. He dared not move, for in the sudden, complete darkness he had forgotten just where that chasm edge had been. Nor, in such darkness, was it easy to remain upright. If, unwittingly, he were to sway a little to right or left, and put out a foot to steady himself —he might step over the edge of the chasm!

'Steady, Jim!' he said to himself. 'Take your time. There ain't nuthin' to get scared about!'

And then he remembered that he had with him in his haversack a small container of paraffin. All he had to do was to remove the cap of the oil-tank of his lantern, do the same with his spare can and pour the paraffin from one into the other: it was as simple as that!

But was it? Simple enough when there was light to work by; but now he must work in the dark. Supposing he missed the orifice in his lantern, and poured the paraffin down the side, over his fingers? It would be lost for ever. And there was not all that much of it to spare. If the paraffin was lost, why, then he, Jim White, was lost too!

With infinite caution, doing his utmost to steady a hand and wrist shaking with the tension of the moment, he applied the lip of the container to the small filler-orifice of the lantern, listening intently for the musical note it should make as it ran in. A little, he was pretty sure, did run in; but his fingers were soon wet, and he knew that he was misjudging the angle and losing precious paraffin as a result. He heard a plop! of paraffin dropping on to the rock at his feet; felt a damp patch on his trouser-leg as it ran down. How much, he asked himself, had he in fact saved?

He cautiously struck a match to find out. Yes, there was a little of the precious fluid in the bottom of his lantern. The wick was fast soaking it up. He lit the wick, replaced the glass, screwed on the cap, and turned round without wasting a second: there might—or might not—be sufficient paraffin for the flame to light him as far as the end of his knotted ropes and, all being well, safety.

He had hardly taken more than half a dozen paces before he heard a tinkle on the floor at his feet and realized that the cap which he thought he had screwed on had fallen off. Stopping with a jerk, he felt paraffin slosh up the side of the container of his lantern. He tore off a piece of his sleeve and rammed it, screwed into a ball, into the hole, then continued on his way. But after a few more paces he remembered how liquids can be sucked up by absorbent material, so he whipped out the piece of sleeve before it absorbed the last precious drops of paraffin—as precious to him as drops of water to someone stranded in the desert.

Luck was with him. Jim White's sense of direction, developed over half a lifetime of cow-punching on the open plain, now stood him in good stead. He regained the end of the tunnel, scrambled up on to the ledge and reached out for the two ends of his knotted rope. And at

that very instant the flame in his lantern flickered for the
second time, and went out. A few seconds earlier . . . Jim
White did not like to think about what would have
happened to him then.

He began to climb, thankful for the big knots he had
had the forethought to make in the ropes. He was climbing upwards this time: not to the broad daylight he had
left but towards a sky that still retained a hint of sunset;
and never before had a hint of sunset seemed so sweet to
him.

He was partway up the ropes when there was a tremendous whirring behind and below him: a terrifying
sound such as he had never heard in all his life before. He
clenched his fists on the ropes and hung there, motionless.
And a few seconds later the strange, ominous, muffled
hissing sound came all about him: he had struck the hour
of the evening exodus of the bats—the very bats whose
strange formation in the sky had brought him out to
explore this slope of the Guadalupe Mountains.

They swept up behind him, between his ropes and the
wall of the shaft, so that the wind of their passing chilled
him. A million tiny whispers surrounded him, a million
tiny clawed wings flapped in the darkness; the air in the
shaft became thick, solid, with their flight, and he felt
himself being suffocated by them and at the same time in
danger of being torn from his precious ropes—his sole
link with the outside world to which he belonged. For the
second time he came near to panic.

Fear, they say, lends wings. It did to Jim White. He
climbed those two knotted ropes almost as fast as the cloud
of insect-hungry bats swarmed up the shaft. He shot up to
the entrance to the shaft as though jet-propelled, to

tumble out over the edge and spread-eagle himself on the rough, rocky slope of the mountainside. Without waiting to untie his ropes, he unhobbled his horse, leapt into the saddle and dug in his spurs: the sooner he was clear of that shaft the better he would be pleased!

Next time he returned to the hole in the mountain-side he had someone with him. Not one of his partners, though. They had laughed at him and refused to believe his story of a shaft, a subterranean tunnel, a cavern beyond that, and a chasm in the middle of its floor which seemed to have no bottom. Instead, he had with him a fifteen-year-old Mexican boy who had attached himself to the ranch and worked there as odd-job boy and general handyman. The men called him 'The Kid'. He did not laugh at Jim White's story, however, but jumped at the invitation to accompany him on a return visit of exploration.

This time they had food and a flask of something to drink. They had two storm lanterns, spare cans of paraffin, a spare axe, all the rope they could lay their hands on about the stockyard and various oddments such as iron bars and hooks. This was to be a major operation, worked out well in advance; it might, they thought, mean three days and nights underground. The two partners grumbled a little at being left to do three-and-a-half men's work between them, but raised no real objection: if Jim and The Kid wanted to indulge in such foolishness, well— jolly good luck to them!

In fact, the three days and three nights very nearly proved their last. They were crawling through a passage when they came upon a skeleton! This astonished the cowboy, and terrified The Kid out of his wits. How ever it got there they had no idea, but the same thought occurred to both of them: someone else had gone exploring—alone —and never returned. Jim recovered from his astonishment. With the idea, perhaps, of bringing it along as a memento with which to persuade his partners of what they had been doing, he detached the skull and slipped it into the knapsack containing their provisions.

As it happened, it was this very skull that so nearly brought about disaster. When he opened the sack to drop it in, he inadvertently loosened the cap of the paraffin container. It began to leak inside the sack. And it could not have done so at a more unfortunate place. For just here they were crawling along a ledge of rock on one side of which was a drop of unknown depth, while on the other a wall of rock rose sheer above them, peppered with jutting fragments of rock, any one of which might have caught in their clothing or the strap which held the sack and jerked them over the edge to their death.

Jim White felt the paraffin seeping from the sack and through his shirt. He could not stop to do anything about it because it was not safe to pause and turn round. Valuable paraffin was being lost. And furthermore, it struck his skin, cold and clammy. But not for long was it cold and clammy. The Kid, close behind him, was holding a torch over his back. A spark fell from it, and immediately set fire to the paraffin-soaked shirt. Jim felt his back on fire. He knew there was a half-opened can of paraffin in the sack; if that caught fire, then it would explode—and that would be the end of them both!

He dared not unbuckle the strap and let the sack fall down the precipice alongside him, for that would mean losing provisions and paraffin too; he could not roll over and extinguish the flames that way, for to roll once would be to roll for the last time; nor could The Kid do anything: he was panic-stricken, helpless with fright. It was a desperate situation for them both.

Somehow, Jim White reached the end of the narrow ledge they were crawling on, without relinquishing his precious load, though by now the pain of his burning back and shoulders was making him gasp. He reached temporary safety and contrived to beat out the flames without damaging the precious container of paraffin. As for his burns, he could do nothing about them: he had not come out equipped with a first-aid kit, so they would just have to mend of themselves. You might have thought that, after the bad luck the skull had brought down upon them, he would have hurled it away into the deepest chasm he could find, glad to be rid of it. But far from it. He hung on to it to the last, and eventually, after spending a number of consecutive days and nights down below, returned to the ranch with a strange tale to tell, and a human skull to show as a memento of an expedition that had so nearly ended in disaster.

Curiously enough, his partners still attached little importance to what he had reported to them. They had enough to do on the ranch, they protested, without messing about in the bowels of the earth! Nor did the odd people to whom Jim White and The Kid talked about their discovery, when they visited town from time to time, seem particularly impressed. Cowboys, they implied, got queer ideas, working out on the open plains beneath a blazing sun all day!

But the time did eventually come when the authorities got wise to the fact that there was money to be made out of this discovery, if it could be skilfully turned to their use. A succession of expeditions, each one better equipped than the last, made the cross-country trip to the slopes of the Guadalupe Mountains and entered the shaft to explore beneath it. Professional photographers, with magnesium-flares and big cameras, sent by the newspapers for which they worked, publicized the cavern-system that was gradually being opened up. Curiosity was aroused far and wide. The notion that there was money to be made out of this natural curiosity was proved to have a good deal of truth in it.

The track worn by the hooves of Jim White's horse and The Kid's pony from the ranch to the opening in the mountainside was widened and signposted. Advertisements were printed in papers all over the States of New Mexico and Texas: 'Visit the Wondrous Carlsbad Caverns!' they said. 'A Subterranean World of Wonder! The Eighth Wonder of the World!' And much more in the same strain.

Was there any truth in what those advertisements promised? Was this something that deserved to rank among the Seven Wonders of the World already accepted? Certainly the hordes of tourists who flocked there to visit the Carlsbad Caverns in ever-increasing numbers year after year were impressed with what they found. And this is hardly surprising, either.

For the Carlsbad cavern system is one of the largest so far discovered anywhere in the world. The total length of the caverns and the tunnels and shafts that interconnect them is over twenty miles, and new lengths continue from time to time to be opened up. What is chiefly outstanding about Carlsbad is the stupendous size of some of the individual caverns, first found by Jim White and later opened up by those who followed in his wake.

They have been given names to match. There is The Cathedral, The Hall of Giants, The King's Palace. But the largest of them all is a cavern that, surprisingly, bears a most uninteresting name: The Big Hall. This is the largest known cavern in the whole world—in volume alone, twenty-five times as large as the next largest cavern so far discovered. It is 2,000 feet long—nearly half a mile; it is 700 feet wide; and very little short of 300 feet high! Such figures are not easy to grasp, however; but an illustration or two may perhaps give some idea of the enormous size of this underground cavern deep down under the Guadalupe Mountains. It covers two acres. It would be possible to set down Windsor Castle, the largest castle in the British Isles, inside this enormous cavern!

As for its height: Nelson's Column, in Trafalgar Square, could stand in the centre of it, and another Nelson's Column on top of that, and even then the great admiral's cocked hat would be well clear of the roof.

Once the entrance had been made simple and straightforward and danger-free, visitors in their thousands flocked to the Carlsbad Caverns. Not for them the knotted ropes hitched to the big boulder, the storm-lanterns and spare cans of paraffin: the authorities opened them up, installed stairways and galleries, flood-lighting, signposts, guides. Handbooks told of the strange layout of the caverns: how some of them were only just below ground level, others 1,000 feet below these—a giant honeycomb with, apparently, no limit in any direction.

As for Jim White: what happened to him? Well, the skull he so obstinately insisted on bringing back with him, though it had so nearly brought about his death and the death of The Kid, brought him eventually a certain measure of good luck. He was granted a concession, and set up a stall at which the thronging visitors could buy food and drink and souvenirs. He set it up at the entrance to the caverns—that very entrance down which he had scrambled on a double-knotted rope, and out of which he had scrambled hot-foot as though Old Nick himself, in the form of a million hungry bats, was after him. And he made a very nice living that way.

He was there as recently as ten years ago or less—half a century almost exactly since he had first approached the mountainside to solve something that puzzled him. He was an old man then, his caving days long past. Visitors who stopped to buy something at his stall, if they had been told who he was, would sometimes question him about his first visit to the Carlsbad Caverns. Was it true that he had entered all on his own? Had he been a bit scared, perhaps? And was it true that he had found a skull down there, and brought it back with him, that time he went down with The Kid?

You can imagine Jim White grinning, and reaching down beneath the counter at which he served food and drink and souvenirs, and coming up with something in his hand, smooth and round and polished, and as white as his name. 'Yup,' he would answer, 'y'can see it for yourself. Here 'tis!'

FOUR: SEARCH FOR A SKIER

ONE fine spring morning in 1948 a well-known skier, Hubert Jungbauer of Linz, waxed his skis, checked his ski-sticks, made up a packet of sandwiches and set off for a long day's cross-country ski-journey on the mountain slopes of the Totes Gebirge, in Austria. They were good ski slopes—if you were an expert; but the region was not popular because it was remote and isolated. Few parties of skiers went there unless they were very keen. It was even more rare for anyone to ski there alone; for obvious reasons.

Jungbauer, however, liked to ski on his own. He was more at home on skis than at the wheel of his car. He preferred that form of activity to all others. One of his reasons for going out on the Totes Gebirge was that he could expect to be on his own all day long. He was therefore not too well pleased when he happened to meet a fellow-skier, also out on his own. Too polite to refuse, however, he agreed to this skier's suggestion that they should make a day of it together.

Perhaps because of a deep-rooted objection to company, which he did not like to put into so many words, after a while Jungbauer mentioned that he proposed to leave the better-known ski-terrain and look for something new. His fellow-skier protested that it was dangerous, but Jungbauer had made up his mind. He set off again, at high speed, slanting away from the direction they had been following until that point. His route now lay diagonally across the mountainside. The other skier was still debating within himself whether or not to go the same way when, to his horror, Jungbauer simply vanished, as though through a trapdoor, in the hard, gleaming snow.

His companion shouted. He followed the track of Jungbauer's skis as far as he dared, and shouted again. There was no reply. Obviously he had fallen into one of the many clefts that were visible on the mountainside in summertime but covered over by snow in winter and spring. Here the snow must have been thin; and Jungbauer's weight . . .

* * * * *

He turned round and sped back to the mountain hut on the Tauplitzalm: there a warden was on duty and could summon a rescue-party by telephone; every second was precious if the lost skier was to be saved before he died of his injuries and exposure in that mountain cleft.

Quickly a rescue-team was recruited. Medical equipment, stretcher, ropes, flexible ladders, lamps, long steel-tipped poles for probing deep snow, hoisting-tackle, crow-bars and other gear were assembled. The members of the rescue-team were all mountaineers, practised skiers, tough and determined. They set off up the mountainside, following the ski tracks, and deployed when they came close to the point at which the ski tracks came to a sudden end. They were roped together, so that if any one of them fell into a crevasse he would be held by the men on either side of him.

A twenty-year-old member of the rescue-party, named Burghofer, volunteered to be lowered through the opening in the snow and down the crevasse on a rope, in an attempt to locate the lost skier. Round his shoulders he carried a coil of light-weight nylon rope with a noose in it; he carried also a torch capable of throwing a powerful beam. His weight was shared by as many men as possible, spread out in an arc so as to distribute the strain on the snow crust.

Burghofer descended 130 feet of almost vertical shaft and then reached a rock ledge with a thin powdering of snow on it. There were traces of blood on snow and rock; and partway down the shaft he had passed a piece of broken ski, sticking out at an angle like a giant thorn. It was quite obvious what had happened: in an attempt to check his headlong fall, Jungbauer had jammed one ski into the wall of the shaft, and it had snapped off. Of the skier himself, however, there was no trace at all.

More rope was lowered down the shaft at Burghofer's request. He could, he said, safely reach the first, possibly the second, of a series of ledges that the beam of his powerful torch had revealed. He continued his descent on a double rope, as a precaution, and ultimately reached a point no less than 600 feet down the crevasse. Here he found a platform of rock large enough for several persons to stand together, if necessary. But even here there was no sign of Jungbauer.

By now, Burghofer was fairly exhausted. He was 600

feet down the crevasse, and had to get up to the top by his
own efforts. It would be touch and go whether he would
be able to grip the ropes with his numbed hands. But he
was tough and eventually reached the top, to make his
report. He had, he said, dropped stones over the edge of
the platform, but had not heard any sound from them: the
bottom of the shaft down which Jungbauer had fallen
must be very deep indeed.

There was now no doubt in anybody's mind that the
lost skier was dead. A series of small expeditions were
organized in the hope of finding and retrieving his body,
but they all failed. Each successive expedition reported
more and yet more tunnels and shafts opening off the
main shaft: it seemed as though it was an underground
labyrinth, and to search them all presented an almost
impossible task.

Three years or so after Jungbauer's death, a really
large expedition was organized, this time by a body known
as the Styrian Caving Group and consisting of highly
experienced pot-holers. Their objective was a twofold
one: to locate the lost skier's body, and to explore and
chart the labyrinth of tunnels and shafts reported by the
earlier expeditions.

They started operations in late summer, when the snow
had melted from the slopes of the Totes Gebirge, though
it still lay in some of the north-facing hollows. Their base
was a substantial mountain hut on the Tauplitzalm Ridge,
three hours' stiff climbing from the valley. To this hut
members of the expedition carried enormous quantities of
pot-holing gear: great rolls of flexible steel-wire ladders
with light-alloy rungs, coil upon coil of climbers' rope,
of varying thickness, telephone-cable and field-tele-

J. M. Dent & Sons Ltd

Entrance to the Gouffre Pierre Saint Martin

Bernard Chandler
Descent of a Yorkshire pot-hole

Main Stream Passage, Peak Cavern, Castleton

Trevor D. Ford

Bernard Chandler

Frieze of deer fording a river, Lascaux Cave

Subterranean river in the Cavern of Montespan

J. M. Dent & Sons Ltd

Ice cavern in the Eisriesenwelt

phones, throat-microphones, junction-boxes, switches
and batteries; canvas sheeting, strong light-weight sacks
for the lowering of equipment to the working-face;
hammers, bars, hooks, grapnels, mountain pitons—strong
shaped pegs for driving into rock to take ropes and
pulleys and flexible ladders; nothing was overlooked.

In charge of the operation was the great pot-holer
Hermann Bock; his second in command was a man
hardly less experienced and capable, Johann Gangl. In
their team were men such as Karl Wiesler, famous guide
as well as expert pot-holer, Hubert Trimmel, Herbert
Franke, who had done pot-holing in many of the world's
limestone regions, and Norbert Zernig who, though he
had had less experience than the others, had already
made a considerable name for himself for his toughness,
stamina and sheer courage.

To reach the pot-hole down which Jungbauer had
fallen to his death more than three years before it was
necessary to climb for two hours after leaving the hut to
which they had carried their main supplies. The area in
which the crevasse was situated was found, when the
snow had cleared, to be a veritable rock colander: there
were great numbers of pot-holes large and small and of
all shapes, all within a comparatively circumscribed area,
known as the Tragelhals, the result, geologists said, of a
major rock fault. Bock and Gangl thought this a possible
advantage: it looked as though there might well be
communication between shaft and shaft, which would
facilitate their exploration.

A cross now stood near the pot-hole down which
Jungbauer had fallen. As Burghofer had reported that
descent below 600 feet looked difficult, if not impossible,

E

it was decided to descend in turn several of the shafts nearest to this, in the hope that there might be lateral shafts along which progress could be made. These shafts were carefully numbered and marked on the large-scale map the expedition was using. There were so many of them that no fewer than forty-three stakes had to be cut and have numbers painted on them before being stuck into the ground close to the pot-holes they represented. The first pot-hole selected for exploration happened to bear the figure '13', and some members of the expedition were superstitious enough to protest. Hermann Bock, however, laughed at them for their fears and refused to change its number. In fact, it did not bring any bad luck with it.

At just short of 150 feet down this pot-hole ceased to be vertical and became an apron of loose and treacherous scree. In spite of the warmth of the August sun on the mountainside the temperature down there was only three degrees above freezing-point. The pioneers of this pot-hole negotiated the scree and worked their way downwards for a further 350 feet. Here they came to a platform from which a whole series of lateral galleries opened out fanwise. The first of these that they penetrated led to a cavern 130 feet long and 170 feet in height; but it proved to be a dead-end. As, in fact, did each successive gallery and chamber explored: beyond each was solid rock, or else a rock-fall too dangerous to negotiate.

So, Pot-hole 13 was crossed off the list. Number 27 was next chosen. The team entered it carrying flexible ladders and lifelines. The leader of this team was Franke. He secured the first ladder to an anchor at the lip of the pot-hole, turned about and began to descend. When he reached a ledge and was able to take his weight off the ladder he signalled up to the entrance and Trimmel clambered down to join him. Together they stood on the ledge, on which a sprinkling of snow still remained, and flashed their torches about them. They were apparently at the base of the shaft, but, as with Pot-hole 13, there were passages radiating laterally from the main shaft, part way up it. One of these looked particularly promising.

Franke climbed back up the ladder a little way, having warned Trimmel to stand clear. He began to swing on it, pendulum-wise, across the width of the shaft until he was able to catch hold of a projecting lump of rock and hold himself still while he prospected. Below him, Trimmel was able to uncover his head, which he had been shielding with his arms while the end of the flexible ladder whipped about in the darkness.

The projecting lump of rock proved to be a sort of threshold to a low and narrow entrance in the side of the shaft. Ducking low, Franke began to work his way into it, head foremost, flashing his powerful torch in front of him to see what was awaiting him. It was another of these lateral passages, right enough. A quick look at his wrist-compass told him that it was running in the right direction: with luck, if it did not come to a dead-end, it might lead him to where he wanted to go.

He called down to Trimmel that he was releasing his hold on the flexible ladder and wanted him to follow him. Then he penetrated the entrance so as to leave the way clear for his companion. But he did not go more than a yard or so; and for a very good reason. Immediately ahead of him there was—emptiness! The lateral passage he had thought he saw was an illusion. He was perching, crouched, on the lip of a vertical shaft of which he could not see the bottom!

Trimmel joined him, using the same pendulum method till he could clutch at the rock and wedge a leg in the opening. Together they contemplated what lay ahead. It was not an inviting prospect: a shaft which opened out almost at once into a chamber. To explore it, a ladder would be required; and they had no spare ladder. But Trimmel had not yet let go of the flexible ladder by which he had joined his leader. They could make use of it, now!

Cautiously they threaded the end of the ladder through the gap and over the lip of this new shaft. The upper end of it of course was still anchored at the surface. But there were many yards of it available, and little by little the two men lowered their ladder into the void until it came taut.

Franke, as leader, took the next step. As before, he turned about and lowered himself over the ledge. To begin with, the ladder hung close against the wall; after twenty or thirty feet, however, the wall receded and Franke found himself hanging free, dangling like a spider on a thread. There was a good deal of sway on the ladder, which was unnerving because he could not know for certain that he would not be bumped against an unsuspected projection and injured, or even shaken from his precarious hold. On the other hand, now that he was clear of the rock wall it was easier to grip the steel wire of the ladder sides without tearing his fingers, and to get a grip on the rungs without stubbing his toes on the rock.

It was dark, though, now. High over his head Trimmel was bending down, trying to steady the ladder and to light his leader's descent; but his lamp was not powerful enough to penetrate such a depth of darkness—darker by far than the main shaft down which they had first descended. Franke was relieved when once again his feet reached solid rock and he could step off his ladder on to another good sound ledge. He called to Trimmel to follow him down.

Once again they stood side by side, considering the next move; and once again Franke announced that he was going on down until he came to the end of the ladder, even though he knew that a tremendous strain was now upon it, since it hung diagonally across the first shaft, was threaded through a tight aperture in the shaft wall, and now slanted downwards in another near-vertical shaft. Before setting off on his next lap, he dropped a stone down below his feet, and listened intently. But the stone could be heard repeatedly striking rock, so it was obvious to them that this next length of shaft, however long it was, must be uneven-sided, perhaps therefore treacherous. As for its depth, they had no means of ascertaining this whatsoever.

Franke left Trimmel on guard: his sole link, now, with those at the top of the main shaft; if anything went wrong, Trimmel would have to act, for he himself would be helpless. In fact, circumstances defeated him: before he reached any further ledge he found that he was stepping off the bottom rung of his ladder—into space! His hands tightened; he lifted his wandering foot back on to the rung it had just left, checked the exclamation that had come to his lips, and began to climb back: whether there was six feet of shaft left, or 6,000 feet, it did not for the moment make any difference.

Next day the pioneer team was reorganized,

strengthened. All the flexible ladders they had brought with them were assembled, together with a supply of rock pitons, additional coils of rope for lifelines, additional lamps. One by one the team descended the main shaft to the point at which the aperture in the rock wall gaped at them; one by one they swung themselves pendulum-wise across the emptiness of the shaft, into and through the gap which Franke and Trimmel had used the day before. Using their strongest pitons, a series of anchors were established, each hammered into the rock until it was immovable, and tested and tested again for rigidity: nothing was to be left to chance.

One by one they worked their way down the second shaft, from ledge to ledge, lowering further ladders, more safety-lines, in front of them to the leaders. With the additional lighting available it was easier to estimate the depth and proportions of the new shaft. But the lamps did little to increase the temperature, which in that deep shaft remained constantly at a degree or two above freezing-point at best. It was so icy cold in the shaft that the moisture of their breath seemed to freeze on their faces so that they felt they were wearing masks; the cold made their sweat cling like an icy undergarment to their bodies. Each man felt he was climbing downwards in a small private world of frost and ice.

Spare lamps were attached to pitons at intervals, casting weird shadows on the walls of the shaft and making them seem more irregular even than they really were. Any pot-holer momentarily caught in their light as he climbed downwards or performed some complicated evolution on the flexible ladders was monstrously dis-torted, his movements exaggerated, so that the whole shaft appeared to be peopled by terrifying creatures from some world in Outer Space.

They came in turn to the ledge on which Franke and Trimmel had stood together. But this time there was plenty of flexible laddering available. More pitons were driven home, more ladders attached to them: several hundred feet of steel-wire ladder and strong lifeline now dangled over the edge of the platform down into the darkness beneath. Once more Franke took it upon himself to lead the descent. After some time he found that the shaft narrowed a good deal; soon it became little more than a fissure in the rock. In spite of this he continued to lower himself, though at intervals he felt as though he was dropping into vertical bottlenecks from which it would be impossible to extricate himself.

At one point in the descent the tube was narrow enough for a boulder to have wedged itself across it from one side to the other. Franke negotiated this by further unrolling the flexible ladder, which had piled up on the boulder, and threading himself down behind it. Then the shaft temporarily widened, and he called on Wiesler, a very experienced pot-holer, to come down after him. Wiesler overtook him and, with permission, passed him at the boulder, to take his turn at leading, for by now Franke was feeling the strain considerably. They came to a further blockage of the shaft, and once again Franke took over the lead.

Then they came to the last rung of the ladder. There were one or two loose stones available, and these they pitched down below their feet, listening intently for the sound they would make on reaching the bottom. Once again it proved impossible to estimate the depth by the sound of the falling stones. They signalled back for more ladders, more pitons, and waited there in the deep and narrow shaft until they came.

One by one the members of the team fed ladders and pitons down the shaft, from stage to stage, till Wiesler could make them fast and lower them to his leader. Meanwhile Franke, who was a keen naturalist as well as pot-holer, gazed round at the walls of the shaft all about him. Here, he realized, was limestone formed aeons ago by the accumulated shells of myriads of creatures who had died, leaving their skeletons and houses to be compressed into rock by sheer weight and the passage of millions of years. The moisture on the walls emphasized the strange and beautiful colours, yellow as well as white and grey, with here and there diagonal bands of pink and palest red: it was a subterranean fairy world.

But a world, as they had eventually to admit, with the greatest reluctance, that seemed to have no bottom. When they had descended to the last rung of their last flexible ladder, they dropped stones into the void, and once again listened keenly. Four . . . five . . . six . . . seven . . . the seconds ticked by, and still there was no sound of the impact of a jettisoned stone on a rock bottom. They realized that to descend further, with these flimsy ladders as their sole link with the upper world, in a shaft so narrow that only one man at a time could make even the slowest progress, was to tempt Providence. Moreover, they were now many hundreds of feet below the point at which, they imagined, the lost skier's body lay invisibly wedged: it was impossible to believe that he could, in free fall, have reached such a depth. And there had been no practicable lateral passages since the last reasonable level. Franke gave the signal that he and Wiesler were beginning their return journey.

One by one the long steel-wire ladders were rolled up, detached from their piton anchors, and conveyed by stages up the shaft to the aperture connecting it with the main shaft, numbered Pot-hole 27. The team came to the aperture, forced their way through it, and one by one climbed the last length of ladder, to step out on the surface. The base party were eager to hear their report, immensely interested to hear of the great depth which they had achieved, sympathetic when they heard that there seemed no further hope of reaching Jungbauer by that means.

This time Johann Gangl, second in command of the Styrian Caving Group, had a suggestion to make: he had been working on the map and consulting with his colleagues, and believed that Pot-hole 38 looked promising. The ladders and ropes were checked for possible fraying or damage from the rock walls, new pitons were assembled to replace those that had been driven into the shafts of Pot-hole 27, and a careful plan of campaign was evolved. Preliminary investigation with weighted cords had given the impression that Pot-hole 38, though vertical, was very deep indeed. Formidable, too; but while even the slenderest chance of finding Jungbauer remained, it must be taken.

His team moved well. A field-telephone had been rigged and a man was kept permanently on duty with headphones on. Progress was reported at intervals. It seemed very little time indeed before Gangl sent up word that he had already reached a depth of 900 feet. He was on a good ledge and was preparing to use a sounding-line

before going any further. A later message told that the
weight on it had run it out to a further 330 feet, and still
had not touched bottom. He was proposing to anchor
more ladders and continue the descent at least to that
level, 1,230 feet below the surface.

Then Nature intervened. Suddenly, without warning, a
thunderstorm broke on the mountainside. Lightning
flashed. The field-telephone apparatus sparked violently,
so that the operator hurriedly pulled off his headphones.
But he replaced them instantly: he was on duty. And his
most important duty at that very moment was to report
down the shaft the conditions at the surface. Glancing upwards at the vast indigo thunderclouds now loading the sky
from horizon to horizon, he knew what might well happen.

Then the rain came. It fell instantly, not in scattered
slanting 'wires' but in solid sheets. The very air turned
grey. The sloping surface of the mountainside was pitted
as though attacked by small-arms fire. And as fast as the
rain fell on to it, it was absorbed, swallowed up, by the
innumerable holes and slits and crevices in the limestone.
That, of course, was the danger. For water can travel
through limestone formations almost as fast as on an open,
unobstructed surface. Down the field-telephone rang the
message: Warning of flood-water! . . . Watch out! . . .
Return immediately!

The message reached Johann Gangl at a depth of
almost 1,000 feet. He and his companions were on a ledge
that appeared to be part of a slanting tunnel. He knew
that flood-water could accumulate in no time at all, and
that when it did move, it could move fast and powerfully.
'Quick! In here!' he commanded; and not a moment too
soon.

For hardly had he and his two companions leapt into a slight hollow in the tunnel wall, their arms linked for additional support, their heels jammed into the rock, when a huge wave of flood-water swept towards them along the tunnel. It was a tidal wave: a flood such as is seen sometimes when the whole sea lifts and bears down upon an unprotected shore, carrying boats high up on to dry land. It snatched at their feet and legs, swirling round them, ripping at them as though determined to snatch them out of their recess and smash them against a rock face or precipitate them down some shaft along the tunnel. The effort to resist the sheer suction power of the water demanded every ounce of strength they possessed.

Fortunately for them underground flood-waters can (though they do not always) subside almost as quickly as they rise: it depends largely on the duration of the storm that causes them. This summer thunderstorm passed swiftly; and as it came at the end of a long dry spell there was not an accumulation of water already in the limestone. And there were many channels and shafts to carry the water away. Gangl and his party felt the level of the flood-water subside. It left their waists, their thighs, their knees; it came down to their ankles. And continued to fall.

For a minute Gangl was tempted to continue his descent; but he put the idea from him: he could not know whether there might be a follow-up to that storm. There might even be delayed-action movement of the subterranean water. He reported back to base that his party was intact, and about to begin its 1,000-foot ascent.

No team could have searched the labyrinthine subterranean passages, tunnels, shafts and caverns of the

Tragelhals more conscientiously, more persistently, than this Styrian Caving Group searched them. But in the end, having explored all the numbered pot-holes large and small, and charted them in detail, they had to confess to failure—in so far as their object had been to locate Jungbauer's body. The lone skier lies where his swift journey ended on that early spring morning twelve years ago. In summertime the strong sun shines down on the mountainside, on the clefts in the limestone so carefully numbered by his would-be rescuers. During late autumn, winter and early spring snow blankets the Totes Gebirge, concealing the clefts from sight of the skier foolhardy enough to take a chance where disaster has already struck.

FIVE: WHERE'S ROBOT?

SUMMER holidays for French schoolboys are very long. So long that many boys get bored as the weeks go slowly by. They run out of ideas for filling-in their time. Only the fortunate ones, whose parents can arrange different occupations for them, changes of scene, a variety of interests, escape being filled with boredom by the time the first seven or eight weeks have gone by. If boys live in some small town, there is not this variety for them; the summer holidays drag interminably.

In the central Place of a small Dordogne town with a very long name—Montignac-sur-Vézère—five schoolboys met one afternoon to discuss how to fill in the rest of the long summer afternoon. '*Je m'étouffe d'ennui!*' said Queroy. '*Moi aussi!*' Estréguil, Coencas and Marcal hastened to agree with him: they too were 'bored to death'.

They turned to Ravidat, the eldest of their little group of five. Perhaps he might have a suggestion to make? Already they had considered and rejected the idea of bathing in the Vézère, which ran close by their homes. It was too hot for any ball game; too hot for gymnastics; too hot even to look out some boy whose leg they could pull, some grown-up they could plague. The fact of the matter

73

was that, down there in the valley where the houses lay, it was too stiflingly, overpoweringly, hot even to think what they would like to do. The four of them waited. Ravidat was sitting in the shade of a tree: perhaps his brain was not yet addled by the heat of the sun?

Between his knees Ravidat held his small wire-haired terrier, Robot. He was panting with the heat, his long pink tongue hanging out beneath his chops. His master was thoughtfully scratching the wiry hair on his forehead: something Robot always enjoyed, even when it was as hot as it was that afternoon.

'It might be cooler up on the hill,' Ravidat said slowly. 'There's usually a breeze up there.'

'Too hot to climb the hill,' Coencas grumbled.

'We couldn't be any hotter,' Estréguil said. 'I think it's a good idea of Ravidat's, don't you, Marcal?'

Ravidat got on to his feet. 'Come on,' he said. 'Robot wants to go, anyway. Look: he's off already!'

The rest of them, grumbling a little, got up too. Soon the little party of five boys and the rough-haired terrier had left the last houses in the town behind them. If any of them had been told that the expedition they were embarking on was to make history they would have laughed at such an idea.

*   *   *   *   *

The two sides of the Vézère valley rise to a great height, and for the most part steeply. They are not smooth, grassy slopes so much as enormous masses of whitish rock piled one on top of the other. From a distance they could almost be mistaken for huge buildings erected on a steep slope: the home of a giant race. Some of the rock masses are vertical; others actually overhang, like the houses built in medieval times, though these are of stone, not timber.

Perhaps castles would be a better comparison. For many of these extraordinary masses of stone look like fortresses, with bastions and turrets and bristling fortifications. One above the other, they soar to the blue sky. And in fact, on the upper reaches men in olden times did build themselves fortified homes, castles with massive bastions and turrets and crenellated walls, in order to achieve security against marauders working their way along the valleys of the Dordogne, the Vézère, the Beune and other rivers that flow through that stony province of France.

But Man had occupied this region of France a long while before the men who built these fortresses. Archaeologists searching for records of Early Man found plenty of relics in the Dordogne, including five skeletons of people —three men, a woman and a child—who had roamed that district as long as 25,000 years before! Cro-Magnon Man, as he came to be known. The authorities demanded that one of the five skeletons should remain in their hands instead of going to the great national museums which ordinarily snap up such important prehistoric relics; as a result, it may still be seen, carefully laid out under a sheet of glass in the village nearest to which it was discovered and laid bare, Les Éyzies, at the foot of a 300-foot cliff of white limestone.

Halfway up that cliff is the local museum, housed in a stone castle. In its showcases may be seen relics of Cro-Magnon Man: his flint weapons, knives, hammers and scrapers, his bone arrows and harpoons and needles. He lived in the Dordogne on and off for something like 10,000 years, at a time when most of Northern Europe was covered hundreds of feet thick in the solid ice that had spread southwards from the ice cap at the North Pole. He had lived with mammoth, wild boar, shaggy bear and bison and the woolly rhinoceros, 25,000 years ago.

The five boys threaded their way through the vineyards that covered the lower slopes of the rocky hillside, Robot bounding eagerly ahead of them all the time. Queroy had called in at his home and picked up his air-rifle: it was always possible that he might be lucky enough to pot a rabbit—perhaps a fox. Robot would ferret them out, if any dog could; and retrieve for him!

Beyond the vineyards the hillside steepened and they had to look out for one or other of the many tracks that criss-crossed one another, worn by peasants who had had occasion to climb to the upper slopes. Every now and then one of the boys would loosen a stone and send it bounding down the track, and call out 'Attention!', so that those behind him would dodge it in time. And every now and then they would come to a halt to recover their breath, and look back wistfully at the blue waters of the Vézère down in the valley at their feet; perhaps after all, they thought as they mopped the sweat off their foreheads, they would have been more sensible to go swimming. Too late for such thoughts now, though; and anyway, there was Robot bounding ahead of them taking short cuts too steep for them to follow on two legs!

The section of the hillside they were on bore the name of Lascaux. Much of it formed part of the estate of the Comtesse de la Rochefoucauld and consisted of scrub oak

and copses of stunted trees that had somehow found root
in the stony soil. There were the ruins of a castle that
some wealthy man had begun to build and then lost
interest in and allowed to fall into decay. The boys had
discovered it several years before, and found it an excellent
place for playing the French version of 'Cops and Robbers'
and similar games. Now they were a little older—
Ravidat was fifteen—they had ceased playing such
childish games, but their old rendezvous was still a
favourite one.

Occasionally in the past some peasant grazing a few
goats had looked suspiciously at them when they turned
up. Grazing on that rough hill slope was free, but what,
he would ask himself, did a bunch of boys want to come
up for, to disturb his beasts? Nowadays, however, no
peasant used it for grazing; and for a very good reason.
A year or two before a precious donkey had been left to
graze there alone. When the peasant had returned to
fetch it, it had vanished. Probably, he thought, in a hole
in the ground that had been left when the roots of a
tree were torn out of it. A rough fence of sticks and
branches and interlaced twigs was erected round it, just
in case some animal strayed that way and was unlucky
enough to fall in. 'Trou de l'Âne,' it came to be called:
'Donkey's Hole'. It was best to avoid it altogether: an
unlucky hole, that Trou de l'Âne!

Panting and out of breath from their climb, Queroy,
Coencas, Marcal, Estréguil and Ravidat dropped to the
ground when they reached the shade of the trees. They
had plenty of time on their hands. There was, as Ravidat
had said, a little breeze up there. Enough to fan them
gently. They had seen no one else on their way up,

F

nothing to pot at with the air-gun. Queroy unloaded it, just to be on the safe side, since it looked as though rabbits and foxes and all other living creatures had decided that it was too hot that day to be out and about. The five of them relaxed in the shade and shut their eyes.

It was not till an hour had passed that anyone noticed that Robot was missing. It did not surprise any of them, for Robot was a restless creature and always up to something. Doubtless he would return when he had satisfied his canine curiosity! However, Ravidat was not entirely happy in his mind: it was unlike his game little rough-haired terrier to stay away so long. Usually he was snuffing around his legs, trying to get his master to come and explore with him. Ravidat put two fingers to his lips and let out the piercing whistle that could be heard right across the valley. That will bring him, he thought. But it did not. Which was surprising. Ordinarily, that whistle had the effect on Robot of a charge of buckshot in his hindquarters, and he would come with a standing jump of about ten feet!

When he had repeated the whistle half a dozen times, and still without any result, Ravidat became worried. As Robot had not come at the call, he must be in trouble. 'I'm going to have a look for him,' he announced to the others. 'I won't be long.'

Some instinct took him in the direction of the Trou de l'Âne. He began to run, whistling at intervals as he ran. There at last it was in front of him: a low fence of twisted branches interlaced with stiff foliage chopped out of the scrub. But he saw immediately that there was a hole in it. It was a triangular patch at the bottom of the fence, at ground level. And he knew at once that it had not been

made by some big animal like a donkey that had charged
into it; rather it had been made by a small animal, low
on the ground, moving fast. He knew at once who that
animal was.

'Robot! Robot!' he called out, throwing himself down
so that his head was almost in the triangular hole.
'ROBOT!'

And this time there was an answer. From far, far away,
it seemed, and deep down below the ground, there came a
muffled yelping which he recognized immediately.

Ravidat was properly alarmed now. Though he had
never seen the Trou de l'Âne at close quarters he knew
that it must be deep; otherwise the peasant would have
found his donkey and extricated it. Waiting long enough
only to shout over his shoulder to the others to come and
help, he began feverishly tearing at the matted branches
and foliage to clear a passage large enough to take his
shoulders. Robot was down there: he must be rescued. He
might be injured by his fall. Ravidat went cold at the
very thought.

By the time the four boys had joined him, the hole was
large enough for him to clamber through. Marcal
pressed forward at his side and the two of them stared
downwards at what confronted them. There was a long
slope of rubble, loose rocks, stones and rock dust running
away from the lip of the hole and vanishing into the deep
shadow cast over it by a precariously balanced boulder on
the upper edge. It looked dangerous. Any sudden or
violent movement, the two boys realized, might dislodge
it. They knew that even a loud voice is capable of setting
off an avalanche of snow in winter-time; perhaps the
same thing could happen to a balanced boulder? They

dropped their voices to a whisper while they discussed their next move.

'I shall go down and find him,' Ravidat said, firmly.

'Roll a stone down, first, to see how deep it is,' Marcal suggested.

'It might injure Robot,' Ravidat answered. 'I myself will find out how deep is the Trou de l'Âne.' And with that he turned round so that his head and shoulders were outside the fence, his body part way through the hole, and his legs dangling down the slope of scree just inside. Queroy joined Marcal as soon as there was room for him, and together, anxiously, they watched their friend begin to slither down and away from them.

Digging his toes in hard, and his elbows too, Ravidat did his best to check the rate of descent. It was difficult, for the rubble and stones were loose and he found himself part of a small avalanche descending the scree. The friction of his body, however, kept him from moving dangerously fast. And all the time he was slithering down he had but one thought in his mind: Was Robot injured? Badly? Soon he would know. The moment did come, however, when the thought occurred to him that it might be more difficult to get out than it was to go in. Ah well: he would have to stay with Robot all night, and in the morning the others would have to climb the hillside again and bring a rope to haul him out with Robot in his arms!

Then he felt his feet touch a surface that no longer moved beneath their weight. His downward motion ceased. Cautiously he straightened his arms, then stood upright. His knees and elbows hurt badly. He could not see much, but when he felt them, he found blood on his fingers. And then, suddenly, there was a wild scampering behind him and he felt Robot's wet tongue feverishly licking his calves. He gathered him up and anxiously felt him all over. No broken bones, thank goodness! Not much wrong with him anyway, to judge by his state of excitement. Good old Robot!

He found that luckily he had a box of matches in his pocket. He pulled out three and struck them in a bunch, to get a better light than with one. The flame revealed that he was in a cave, with walls of solid rock. It was, he guessed, about ten yards from side to side; but it must be a good deal longer than that because the far end was still in shadow. Satisfied now that his dog was not injured, Ravidat's next thought was to call his friends down to see what he had found.

'*Venez—vite!*' he shouted up to them. '*Venez!*'

They did not need a second invitation. Already Marcal was slithering down the scree, using his stomach as a toboggan, grunting with annoyance as the rough stone tore his knees and elbows. Queroy was close behind. Then Coencas, with Estréguil immediately after him. Soon all five of them were standing shoulder to shoulder on the gritty floor, with Robot jumping excitedly about among their feet. Four of them had boxes of matches. They lit them, as Ravidat had done, in bunches of three or four. By the combined illumination of the flares they realized that the cave they had discovered was at least twice as long as it was broad, and that its roof of solid rock rose above their heads in a great arch like the curved roof of a church.

The light was strong enough to dispel shadows, but nevertheless shadows seemed to remain here and there on the walls of the cave. Then their matches went out. At

Ravidat's bidding, however, they lit further bunches of matches: something about those shadows—if they were in fact shadows—had aroused his curiosity. As soon as all their matches were alight he made for the nearest wall, beckoning to the others to come too. And what they now saw by the combined light of all their matches took their breath away.

For these were not shadows at all. Right up to the curved roof over their heads the walls of the cave were covered thickly with monstrous animals painted in black and brown and yellow and red! As well as horses, oxen, stags and bulls there were horned animals which they did not recognize. They were large and small, running, fighting, charging, poised to charge, resting, leaping—in all sorts of positions, singly and in groups large and small.

Unable to believe their eyes, they held the matches up to the walls until they burned their fingertips. Even then they were too excited at their unexpected find to feel any pain. Hurriedly they lit more matches, and yet more matches, impatient to see all that there was to see. The drawings and paintings were unlike anything else they had ever seen in their lives. Some of them were as much as fifteen feet in length. Some were outlined in bold black lines and coloured red or yellow or brown inside; others had no outlines but were made up of two or more colours; and all of them seemed to shine in the faint yellow light of the matches, almost as though they had been glazed over. When at last Queroy took courage and put out a hand to touch one of the painted figures, he found that the surface, though it undulated and curved quite a bit, was as smooth as glass.

The last of the matches, except a few that Ravidat had

wisely kept in reserve for an emergency, burned out. Darkness closed in upon them again. The only glimmer of light came from the end of the cave by which they had entered, filtering towards them down the slope of scree. They remembered, suddenly, that that was their only way out; and as suddenly they all knew that what they wanted most of all to do was to get back home, collect torches and some rope and return as soon as possible to try to solve the mystery of the cave for themselves.

Ravidat organized their return up the scree. The smallest boy must go first; behind him, the next in size, boosting him upwards and making what progress he could himself. Then the next in size, and the next in size; and finally himself, with Robot. Estréguil, the fourth in order, worked his way up more or less alongside Ravidat, with Robot scrambling furiously between them, impatient to be out of the cave, and of course not having the slightest idea that he himself was responsible for all this excitement of discovery.

The five of them were back next day, complete with torches, spare batteries and some rope. It was as hot as ever, but they hardly noticed the heat as they raced up the stony hillside that towered above the town of Montignac-sur-Vézère. Quickly they anchored one end of the rope to a good sound root, threw the loose end down the slope of scree and scrambled one after another down it and into the cavern to which it was the difficult doorstep. Now for real exploration!

The cavern proved to be some sixty feet long by thirty feet wide at the end near the scree. But it tapered inwards until at the further end it was little more than a cleft in the rock. Part way along the right-hand wall, though,

there was a gap. This they penetrated, Ravidat in the
lead, shining his torch forward, Queroy and Estréguil
close behind him, each lighting up one wall of the passage
in which they found themselves, and Coencas and Marcal
in the rear. They moved forward cautiously, remembering
that one hole in the ground had already proved treacherous; they did not want to be caught napping by another!

After a while they came to a 'T'-junction. To the left
there was a small chamber, to the right a larger chamber.
It took only a minute or so to realize that to the left it
was a dead end: no more than a cleft in the rock. But the
other was much more promising. Not only was it much
larger, but towards the far end there was an opening in the
floor which clearly led somewhere.

They dropped to their knees round the opening and
pointed their five torches downwards. And there they saw
a substantial 'staircase' of loose stones slanting downwards
at a guess as much as thirty feet or more: they could not
see the end of it from where they were kneeling.

Ravidat and Estréguil looked at one another: this was
something too good to miss. If only they had had the
sense to bring down with them their spare coil of rope,
they would have a shot at it right away. Marcal volunteered to go back to the foot of the scree and fetch it.
Coencas was told to accompany him: no one, Ravidat
ordered, was to go anywhere in this cave *on his own*. He was
a good leader, and aware of his responsibilities towards
the others, who were a year or so younger than he.

The spare rope arrived. Ravidat quickly made a noose
and threw it round his chest close beneath his armpits.
Estréguil was to stand by; the three others were responsible for hanging on to the rope. They were to wedge

themselves so that, however great the strain on the rope might be if something gave way and all his weight came suddenly on it, they could hold him. Then he began to lower himself on the rope, testing the 'anchor' as he went. After thirty feet or so he found himself on a level rock floor again. He slipped out of the noose and called to the others to haul it in so that Estréguil could join him.

Then they flashed their torches round this new cavern-beneath-a-cavern. Here too were paintings of animals that covered the walls to the arched roof above their heads, each more exciting than the last. They could hardly contain their excitement. Generously, Ravidat swarmed back up the rope and sent the three others down, one at a time, while he remained on anchor for their safety.

They returned next day, and the next, and the day after that. By the end of the fifth day they had explored every nook and cranny of the complex network of subterranean chambers and passages leading from one to another on different levels. Here and there they had encountered great piles of debris, where rock had broken away from a fault in the roof and spilled down on to the floor beneath, barring further progress along some passageway. It is possible that the thought occurred to one or other of the boys: supposing that were to happen just after we had gone along the passage, what would become of us? But if so, no one mentioned his thoughts to anybody else, at least until they had emerged safely from the exit to the Trou de l'Âne!

So far they had said nothing about their discovery to anybody in the town. But one evening Ravidat, turning over the pages of an encyclopaedia, saw a reference to a cavern near Santander, in Spain, where extraordinary

rock paintings had been discovered. There were pictures
of some of them. He knew then that it was time they told
someone about their discovery. For the encyclopaedia
made it very clear that those other rock paintings were
very important indeed; archaeologists had come from all
parts of the world to examine them and as a result had
been able to fill in a blank chapter of prehistory.

The obvious person to tell was their schoolmaster,
M. Léon Laval. At first he would not believe them; he
suspected that it was a practical joke of a kind a little
more elaborate than those which his schoolboys were
accustomed to play on him. But Ravidat was a boy whom
he respected; and he was obviously completely sincere as
he made his report. Besides, when the other boys offered
their individual stories in confirmation of what their
leader had said, all the details tallied one with another.
M. Laval was finally convinced; and being convinced,
lost no time in communicating the news to the greatest
French archaeologist of his day, one of the greatest
scholars of prehistory in the world, the Abbé Breuil.

One week later, less than a fortnight after the small
rough-haired terrier had tumbled down the scree into the
Trou de l'Âne, a party of archaeologists, led by the
famous Abbé Breuil himself, descended on the sleepy
little riverside town of Montignac-sur-Vézère to see the
cavern for themselves. It took them a long time to climb
the hillside, escorted by Ravidat and his four school
friends and their schoolmaster. Workmen had cut steps in
the scree, and reinforced them with strong stakes. It was
easier, now, to descend than it had been that first time.
And when they had descended, and flashed their torches
round the walls and roof of the first cavern, and then of

the second cavern, they knew at once that what they were looking at was among the most important archaeological discoveries ever made. The only other wall paintings that began to compare with these at Lascaux for beauty and originality were those found in the cavern at Altamira, near Santander, in northern Spain.

Above all they were excited by the very last of the paintings the boys had discovered. They had already been impressed by the great bulls painted on the domed roof, whose horns almost interlocked; by the flotilla of stags painted swimming across a river; by an extraordinary monster with a humped neck and two straight horns that thrust outwards and upwards unlike those of any horned beast ancient or modern that they had ever seen, and with large black spots and circles painted all over its body. But what astonished them and fired their imagination most of all was an 'action'-picture—the oldest ever discovered, and going right back to the Paleolithic Age.

An 'action'-picture, as it were, tells a story. This one certainly does. The painting presents a group. On the right of it is a magnificent bison, about to collapse as the result of a great wound in its belly through which its guts are dangling down. Near the bison's head is a long, straight 'stick'-man such as children draw today. He is falling stiffly backwards, apparently having been gored to death by the bison in its own death agony. He is obviously a hunter because a javelin is sticking into the bison, and the javelin throwing-stick, with its bird-mascot head, has fallen to the ground beside the hunter after use. The hunter's arms are outspread as he falls.

But there is another figure in the group: a triple-horned

rhinoceros which can be seen lurching away to the left of the picture. It is obviously the rhino that has ripped the powerful bison's belly with its cruel horns, for the hunter's javelin would not have been capable of making such a terrible wound. So here is a tragedy: a bison mortally wounded by a rhino has in turn mortally wounded the hunter whose work was done for him by that great lumbering triple-horned monster—who himself has got away scot-free!

The Abbé Breuil and his team of experts were able to establish that these rock-paintings were the work of Cro-Magnon Man, who had roamed the valleys of the Dordogne about 25,000 years ago. Other prehistoric paintings had of course been found elsewhere, but none of them offered 'action'-pictures such as this. The ability to portray animals in action like this proved that Cro-Magnon Man was a much more highly developed creature than had once been believed. As well as being a great hunter, he was a considerable artist. He had flourished at a time when one of the terrible Ice Ages was blotting out much of Europe. He had established himself, fought wild animals for living-space, survived the bitter cold of the glaciers as they slid downwards from the mountain slopes, and left deep down underground these memorials of his way of life. And none of these, to this day, might have been discovered had it not been that some twenty years ago a group of restless schoolboys, bored at the end of their long holidays, lost their rough-haired terrier Robot and went in search of him in the Trou de l'Âne.

six: SUBTERRANEAN ICE

'IT CAME snarling at me like a beast of prey!' the man said. 'Frightened? I should say so. I was terrified out of my wits. I wouldn't go back up there, not for any money in the world!'

The man who said that was a hunter of chamois, a man well used to danger and hardship. His hunting-ground was on the steep slopes of the Salzburg Alps, where to have any chance of getting within range of the nimble and surefooted chamois a man had to be not only strong but as agile as an acrobat.

His friend nodded. He knew his man; knew that he was not given to exaggeration: there must be something in his story for him to say what he had just said. But another man, an acquaintance of his, had heard only the last remark. He came across, curious to know what it was all about. 'Wouldn't go back up where, for any money in the world?' he asked.

The hunter turned to him, glad to have an increase in his audience. 'I was after chamois,' he said. 'It was quiet enough, up there on the Alps. No wind, for a change. I turned a shoulder of the mountainside, though, and all of a sudden I heard a furious snarling, menacing, shrieking noise like nothing I'd ever heard before.'

'What did you do?' His audience looked at him expectantly.

'Do? Well, after recovering from my surprise I set off to locate the source of the snarling sound. And, guess what? I came to the entrance to a cave on the mountainside, and out of it there came a mighty rushing wind, a fair tornado of a wind, that struck me full and nearly threw me over. And I'll tell you another thing: that tornado of snarling wind was as cold as ice!'

His audience was impressed. A 'snarling tornado': well, that was certainly something new! Curious that no one else had reported it. But then, where the chamois were to be found it was pretty rough going; no one was likely to go that way just for a stroll! It sounded cold, too. . . .

*   *   *   *   *

The story of the ice-cold, snarling wind and the cave mouth high on the mountainside spread around the district. One man whose ears it reached was a mountaineer, a naturalist and one of the first men ever known to interest themselves in subterranean exploration—for this episode took place eighty years ago. His name was Posselt-Csorich. Being curious to get to the bottom of this strange report, he took steps to track down the chamois hunter, located him and promised to reward him handsomely if he would act as his guide and take him to the cave high on the slopes of the Salzburg Alps.

Together they climbed the mountainside. It was steep and the going was treacherous as well as arduous. The chamois hunter climbed fast, anxious to get the job done and collect his reward. Soon they reached an altitude of

5,380 feet. And there was the cavern entrance: seventy feet high and nearly as wide, its floor covered with enormous boulders.

Nor had the chamois hunter exaggerated when he spoke of the snarling tornado that came from it. A torrent of ice-cold air flooded out from the cave mouth, emitting a rising-and-falling, banshee-like wailing sound as though all the tormented spirits in the Hell of old mythology were shrieking in their eternal agony. It might well be, Posselt-Csorich reflected as he stood there, the very mouth of Hell!

But he stood there alone. For the chamois hunter, having fulfilled his promise, demanded his reward and set off back home as hard as he could go: this was no place for him! Courageously, Posselt-Csorich decided to enter the cave mouth. The wind, which as he ascended the last few hundred feet of the mountainside had sounded louder and louder, now not only roared and wailed in his ears but seemed to pummel and punch him like a live creature. He felt himself enveloped by it, enveloped and almost overwhelmed. His feet were almost snatched from underneath him; he had to lean forward, clutching on to whatever offered temporary support.

Little by little, keeping as much as possible to one side, out of the main stream of the wind, and clutching his jacket about him to stave off the cold, he worked his way forward. He surmounted the first slope of treacherous boulders and rubble. Loose stones fell away beneath his feet, he stumbled and barked his shins, his knees, his elbows, and tore his hands and fingernails as he strove to get a grip on the loose surface. More than once when he fell his oil-lamp went out and had to be relit. And the fourth time he relit his lamp he realized that he had done so only just in time. For he found himself perched at the top of a huge landslide of loose rocks: emptiness before him, and emptiness above and on each side of him.

He knelt there, motionless, until his eyes had accustomed themselves to the change in the darkness: a subtle and mysterious colour in the darkness his small, inefficient lamp did so little to dispel. He turned up the wick as far as he dared, and shone his lamp in all directions. He realized that he was in a vast cavern whose roof was too high above his head to be seen; but it was a cavern different from any he had ever been in, or even dreamed of, in all his life before.

It was a cavern of—green ice! Ice for the floor; ice for the walls; ice, he believed, because of the stalactites that hung down from it within the range of his lamp, for the roof. Gigantic ice pillars, stalagmites, rose all about him from the ice floor into the emptiness above him, as though designed to support an arch that itself supported a whole mountain-top. The whole vast cavern seemed to be shimmering: though whether it was the shimmer of cold light, or the effect of the snarling wind that surrounded him and filled the whole interior to bursting-point, he could not say.

Most pot-holes, of course, tend to be colder than the world outside. No mountain pot-holer is surprised at having to work in a temperature perhaps not many degrees above freezing-point. The hard rock on which he places his hand will often be cold enough to numb his fingers so that he has difficulty in gripping ropes and flexible ladders and other tackle. If he comes up against water, either as a stream or as spray from some cataract, it will seem to him as cold as ice; the spray hanging in the air will be icy cold. And of course this must involve an additional hazard: the ice will be far more slippery even than wet rock. To walk along a level tunnel will be difficult; to ascend a gentle slope even more difficult; to descend a gentle slope more difficult still. To pass through crawls and squeezes, up and down vertical or steeply slanting shafts, will call for skill and stamina as well as mere strength and courage. To slip and fall may mean a broken limb; and that means an underground rescue in the worst possible conditions.

It was into such a cave-system that, without fully appreciating it at the time, Posselt-Csorich was making a pioneer survey. For this was the famous Eisriesenwelt, in the Tennen Gebirge range, not far from the town of Salzburg. Of all the ice caves so far discovered in Europe it is the most impressive. It is by far the largest, the coldest, the most labyrinthine, and one of the most difficult to penetrate and chart; and so, for those very reasons, among the most rewarding to the very keen pot-holer. Its name means the World of the Ice Giants.

Posselt-Csorich advanced with extreme caution into the unknown. The ice beneath his feet was so slippery that even the nails of his mountain-climber's boots did not prevent him from falling over and over again. The floor sloped slightly downwards, which made progress more difficult rather than easier. Almost every time he fell his oil-lamp went out and had to be relit: and each time he relit the lamp the scene in which he found himself appeared stranger and stranger. The cavern walls glittered with a myriad crystals and took on weird colours from the yellow flame of his lamp; the sheen on

G

the smooth ice floor sometimes made it look as though it was the surface of an ocean, sometimes as though he was walking over fire. And all the time the ice-cold wind roared past him, so deafening him that he found it almost impossible even to think.

In spite of this, in spite of the fact that he was alone, Posselt-Csorich pressed onwards resolutely. But when he had covered what he estimated to be a quarter of a mile or more, he found himself confronted by a colossal ice-covered mass of rock that apparently blocked the whole end of the cavern. Try as he might, he could find no way round it on either side; to clamber up and over it, without ropes and tackle, was clearly impossible; yet, since the wind was coming with tremendous force from the far side of it there *must*, he told himself, be an opening beyond it.

Reluctantly—or perhaps not entirely with reluctance—Posselt-Csorich turned back. And for one reason or another he never repeated his visit to the Eisriesenwelt. In fact the cavern was not revisited for something like thirty years; this time by a young art student named Alexander von Mork who happened to have come across Posselt-Csorich's account of his lone exploration in a journal of mountaineering. Why, he asked himself, had he never heard of this strange ice cavern before? No one, it seemed, had been back there; at least, no one had published an account of it. So he might as well have a shot at rediscovering it for himself!

Von Mork told a few of his most active student friends. They collected the sort of equipment they thought most likely to be of use in such unusual conditions: steel-tipped staves, ice-picks and ice-axes, as well as lengths of rope.

They got hold of climbers' crampons for their boots, with the idea of moving more safely over ice, as mountaineers did on frozen snow. They had acetylene lamps, which not only gave an infinitely better light than the old-style oil-lamp, but were less likely to go out with rough usage. Before entering the cavern they even worked out and memorized a system of signalling by lamp flashes as well as using the established rope signals. They left, so far as possible, nothing to chance.

As Posselt-Csorich had said, there was no way round the massive block that filled the end of the enormous cavern a quarter of a mile in from the entrance: it must, therefore, be surmounted. They attached climbing-irons to their boots and, working in relays, proceeded to cut a series of steps in the face of the block, finding the ice that coated it as hard almost as steel. The chips that flew from the ice-axes were dangerous and could easily blind anyone who was unlucky enough to be hit by them.

Von Mork took the lead on the last stretch of step-cutting. They had now reached the upper slope of the block and found themselves close against the roof. The most formidable element, however, was the wind. For this was coming towards them in a thin, violent sheet through what must be a wide but low slot that compressed it and allowed it to come through in a burst of power that made it almost impossible to withstand. The cold of this fast-moving stream of air made it cut like a scythe. The sound of it—now a high-pitched scream—was deafening; it seemed to belabour their heads and knock them about.

But at least they had established that there was a way through beyond the rock. For safety's sake they now roped up. Then, moving laboriously in single file, carrying their gear as best they could with numbed hands, using their ice-picks to give them steadiness as they climbed, they worked their way forward and over the top of the ice-covered boulder until they came to the lip of the orifice through which the wind came charging out like a dragon of ice. The ceiling was so low, now, that they had to kneel down. But one by one, with von Mork in the lead, they forced their way through the passage in spite of the terrible wind, breasting it as a surf-rider breasts the surf as he makes his way out into deep water before turning to ride triumphantly back to the beach.

Von Mork, in the lead, eventually found himself in another and even larger cavern; or rather, as it was soon to be revealed to him, the first of a series or network of caverns, all of them floored and walled and roofed with gleaming ice. It was almost unbelievable: a fairyland, a wonderland beneath the land, filled with colours such as he had never seen in any of the art books he had studied, in any of the paintings in the great art galleries he visited, or on the brushes and palettes of any of the painters whose work he had ever seen.

He was joined in due course by the rest of his small team. Being young, they gloried in the fact that they were the first ever to enter this cavern, for they knew that Posselt-Csorich had been forced to turn back at the barrier. This new cavern was so vast that the combined light from their powerful acetylene lamps failed to reach the roof or even to the further end. Enormous pillars of ice, which they estimated at a hundred feet and more, soared into the darkness beyond the range of their lamps. Some of the pillars were straight, like those in a great cathedral;

others were weirdly shaped, bulging here, narrowing there, twisted like sticks of giants' barley sugar, distorted like aged forest oaks: it was as though these had been so plucked at by the raging, relentless wind that they had had no chance to grow as pillars should. And as they moved their lamps here and there, vast shadows were cast on the ice walls, and the twisted, contorted columns appeared to writhe, like giants in the agony of death. The very air of the cave, ice-cold to breathe, seemed to be alive and threatening revenge for the invasion of this sanctuary.

They remained roped up as they began to advance again: there was no telling what hazards lay ahead. For a time the floor ran level: slippery and hazardous but beautiful in the light of their combined lamps. The wind still roared past them, but on a lower note, now that they had passed through the narrow rock gap. And then, unexpectedly, they came to a lake that extended over the greater part of the cavern floor. It was not frozen, as they could tell from the wavelets whipped to a frenzy by the wind sweeping over its surface. They tried to estimate its depth with their ice-picks, and von Mork even ventured a little way into the water. But the floor dipped and he realized that even if it levelled out, the water was so cold that his legs might freeze. Defeated for the time being, they returned by the way they had come.

Some weeks later von Mork and his two closest companions, Angermeyer and Rihl, returned. Since it was obviously impracticable to transport a boat over the ice block and through the narrow windswept gap, they had brought diving-suits. They stood on the edge of the lake. The waves looked bigger than they had done the first

time, lashed by the wind, reaching out towards them as
though determined to bowl them over and then drown
them. Angermeyer and Rihl helped von Mork into his
diving-suit, buttoning it closely round his neck and wrists
and ankles and then attaching him to themselves by a
length of rope with a loop round his chest.

Von Mork stepped into the icy water, his friends paying
out the rope very slowly, so that it was never entirely
slack: they might at any moment have to heave on it to
extricate him from some unseen hollow in the rock floor.
He found the water less deep than he had feared; but
colder than anything he had ever experienced. After the
first few yards it was well up his calves, the wave-crests
beating at his knees. The diving-suit was less efficient than
he had expected, and almost immediately he felt the icy
water seeping in round his ankles. Soon his feet were
chilled to the bone. Numbness crept up his legs. Muscles
on which he had relied began to stiffen. It was as though
they had been seized in clamps and the screws remorse-
lessly turned. He lost all feeling in the lower part of his
legs; except for the agonizing cold that embraced them it
was as though he was walking on stilts.

He succeeded, through indomitable will-power, in
crossing the lake to the further side. The water had never
come higher than mid-thigh, and by then he had lost all
feeling in the upper part of his legs too. There had been
one really bad moment when the ice-coated roof had
come low over his head and he had had to wade while
bent almost double, his chest on the surface of the lake.
After that he was numb all over. With stiff fingers he
tried to pinch himself—and felt no pain at all, hardly
even any pressure!

But he stepped out into yet another magic world, if possible lovelier than anything he had seen before. Fearful that he might collapse of sheer numbness, however, he remained there only long enough to establish the fact that from that point onwards there was a labyrinth of passages so complex that it could only be explored by a well-organized party, with much better equipment than he and his friends possessed. Even a quick glance showed him that there were any number of ways in which a party might lose its members down here, deep down under the ice roof, if they did not have staging-points and lifelines and plenty of lighting. Meanwhile, he had to cross that icy lake again to rejoin his companions: he even wondered whether his numbed limbs would respond to the demands he would have to make on them. One thought buoyed him up, however: he would do his utmost to be included in the bigger and better-organized expedition which would come here next.

He was unlucky. Von Mork was killed in battle during the First World War. It was twelve years and more before Angermeyer and Rihl were able to get a group of experienced pot-holers interested in the Eisriesenwelt. But when at last they did enter the cavern they brought von Mork's ashes with them in a beautiful marble urn and Angermeyer and Rihl reverently placed it on a great stone slab like an ice-covered altar in the cavern von Mork had been the first to enter. Thereafter it bore his name in the charts: Alexander von Mork Dome.

A number of well-organized groups of pot-holers climbed the 5,380 feet of mountainside between the two world wars, each better equipped than the last. Their leaders bore names famous in the pot-holing world:

Hermann Gruber, Friedrich Oedl, Gustav Abel and
Walter von Czoernig-Czernhausen. They carried, in
addition to the usual gear, surveying instruments such as
theodolites with which to chart every inch of this extraordinary labyrinth of caves, passages, shafts, funnels and
tortuous crawls and squeezes of which von Mork had
obtained only an inkling. Each successive penetration
revealed more labyrinthine ways. It was necessary to rig
guide-lines as well as lifelines, to have well-mounted stage-
posts, so that no group was ever out of touch with its
base.

Eventually no fewer than twenty-five miles of subterranean passages interlocking the caverns had been
penetrated, explored, surveyed and charted, often in
conditions of great difficulty and danger. Beyond the last
tortuous passage, the last cul-de-sac and dead end, the
last constricted ice cave, the last precipitous shaft and
deadly tunnel walled with ice and swept by icy wind,
they came up against a final and truly impenetrable wall:
the very core of the Tennen Gebirge beneath which this
labyrinth sprawled. It was estimated that something like
23,000 square yards of tunnel and passage made up this
world-beneath-a-world; and many of them sheeted with
hard, impenetrable ice.

The map that was eventually drawn resembles as much
as anything a frayed piece of coarse twine that has been
unravelled and twisted up and unravelled again and
again. There are thick, bulging lengths of it representing
such great caverns as those first penetrated by Posselt-
Csorich and by the young art student von Mork thirty
years later; thin strands represent the interminable
cramped corridors linking cavern with cavern; spidery,

angular sections represent the short passages without
exits, zigzagging through the rock, in which a man might
lose his nerve and die of exhaustion and exposure before
being located. The Eisriesenwelt is a death-trap fashioned
in hard green ice.

It may be wondered how so much was discovered when
a lake of ice-water lay in front of it. The lake was found
to vary a good deal in depth: proof that it was fed from
some outside source of supply. It had only to become a foot
or two deeper than it was when von Mork crossed it
to become impassable for men carrying gear. Drastic
measures, until then unique in the history of pot-holing
and rarely if ever used since, were taken. A suitable outlet
for the lake waters was found in the form of a big rock
fissure on the other side of the barrier. Explosive was
brought into the cavern. The rock was drilled and
splintered with powerful wedges. The charges were inserted and the fuses lit. Everyone, including the mining
engineers who had been co-opted to undertake this
difficult and dangerous feat, took cover. There followed
the roar of the explosion, a sound which hammered at
their eardrums and reverberated for a long while through
the caverns and tunnels, drowning even the furious
howling of the wind. When the explorers emerged from
their hiding-places it was to find that the waters of the
lake were fast draining away; soon there was only a series
of puddles left in the hollows in the rock floor and the
way was clear to go forward.

Such a cave-system deserves to have been not only
charted but given names to its component parts that
match them in evocative power. You will find such names
here in the Eisriesenwelt. The first great cavern, into

which Posselt-Csorich ventured alone, having been
deserted by the chamois hunter, is named after him:
Posselt Hall. Beyond it, beyond the rock and ice barrier
that defeated him but was conquered by a small party of
young students, is a cavern named Hymir's Hall, taking
its names from a character in old Norse mythology telling
of Odin, Thor and the other Scandinavian gods and
goddesses and giants. In this enormous cavern is a rock
and ice formation rising to the roof, battlemented and
turreted: it is appropriately named Hymir's Castle.

Beyond this come the Ice Gates, and then Mork's Dome.
Then comes the beginning of the real labyrinth, its
sections variously named: Tube Labyrinth, Canyon
Labyrinth, Odin's Hall, Friga's Veil, the Castle of the
Gods, Asenheim and Niflheim.

But there is labyrinth upon labyrinth: as so often, the
caves and passages have been carved on different levels.
No less than 400 feet above the level of the entrance to
the Eisriesenwelt, itself between 5,000 and 6,000 feet
above sea level, there is the great hall named after the
Norse Giant of Storms, Thyrm. Here the snarling wind
roars everlastingly through its emptiness, channelling off
among the passages on either side, up and down the shafts
with their ice-coated sides. The name was well chosen, in
this case!

Beyond the first labyrinth comes another, no less
complex, no less hazardous to explore and chart. Here are
to be found the Hall of Separation, ominously named; the
Vault of Terror, the Gallery of Bats, the Diamond
Kingdom, Dripstone Tunnel, Rockfall Chamber, Mount
of Fools, Frau Oedl Vault and Poldi Vault; there are other
named sections of this great and formidable labyrinth.

Nearly half a mile into the mountain from Posselt Hall is another labyrinth. It contains one of the largest of all the subterranean caverns, the Ice Palace. Opening off it is a tangle of passages large and small: Slippery Tunnel, Stalactite Dome, Avalanche Dome (another grim reminder of unexpected accidents), the Dome of Terror and Vertical Canyon. Robert's Drop is there, too: a name that tells a story in two brief words. Rub out all those names and start again on the chart of the Eisriesenwelt, and you will find as many names again, and yet again: and all of them with a reason.

After many years of exploration and charting, this vast system of rock-and-ice-filled caves has now been probed to its final secret and mystery. Or, perhaps, its last mystery but one. What is the source of the snarling tornado of wind that first frightened the chamois hunter eighty years ago, intrigued Posselt-Csorich soon afterwards, and buffeted the young art student von Mork and his fellow students when they went in some thirty years later? Every successive expedition has had to contend with it; they found it possible to drain off the ice waters of the underground lake, to chart the labyrinth of passages and tunnels and shafts; but they never solved the mystery of the source of that terrible ice-cold wind, the original and permanent inhabitant of the Eisriesenwelt. Perhaps the Norse Giant of Storms, the tempestuous Thyrm, knows the answer; but his voice is too loud, too blustering, too violent, for anyone to translate him when—if ever—he condescends to give it.

SEVEN: KILLER CAVE

Ten years or so ago a small group of pot-holers were scrambling among the crags that mark the frontier between France and Spain, 6,000 feet up on the Pyrenees, a mountain range whose summits rise to 11,000 feet. One of them, a man named Lépineux, was not only—like all climbers—an extremely observant man; he was also something of an ornithologist. Though only an amateur, he knew more than a little about the ways of birds.

The party had sat down to rest between one bout of scrambling and the next. Some were munching sandwiches, others smoking; they were tired, but relaxed; perhaps they would do another stiff scramble that afternoon; perhaps they would descend to the valley, content with what they had already achieved. Meanwhile they looked about them. It was a barren scene: limestone crags and pinnacles, a good many formidable-looking crevices in the stone, which they avoided as far as possible, and hardly a tree in sight, for the soil was too thin to support even the hardy mountain pine except in an occasional hollow where it had accumulated in greater depth. Only keen pot-holers would have taken any pleasure in being on that particular stretch of the Pyrenees.

'*Regardez!*' one of the men said, suddenly. The rest of the party looked keenly in the direction to which his hand was pointing. A large black mountain crow had shot suddenly out of what appeared to be solid rock.

The majority of the party was surprised, but not particularly impressed. 'So what?' was their reaction. They returned to their sandwiches, wondering why anyone should have thought it worth commenting upon. But one of their number was interested: Lépineux.

'That's curious!' he remarked. '*Très curieux!*'

'What's so curious?' someone asked him.

'When that crow appeared, it was already in full flight. It has its nest somewhere near what must be a deep hole—that means—a pot-hole!'

Lépineux got to his feet. 'Anyone coming?' he asked. One or two of the others joined him. They set out in the direction in which they had seen the unexpected bird. It involved quite a climb up the side of a combe, or, as the combe is called in those mountains, a *cirque*. It was rough going, but they came at last to a *doline*: a cone-shaped depression with a shaft slanting very steeply indeed into the side of the *cirque*. It was narrow, forbidding; its rim consisted of heavy pieces of limestone insecurely balanced and wedged. Only a winged creature might hope to enter or leave it with any feeling of safety at all. 'Nasty!' was the comment Lépineux and his companions made. 'Someone else can have the pleasure of descending that; not me!' Lépineux added.

*   *   *   *   *

In August 1951 a team of twelve expert pot-holers was organized and equipped: their objective was to plumb

the depths of a pot-hole which, from its position close to a
frontier stone on the Franco-Spanish border, came to be
known as the Gouffre Pierre Saint-Martin. Little did they
know, when they began their first descent, that not
merely days, weeks or even months would elapse before
the last secrets of this formidable pot-hole were laid bare:
it was to be a matter of years! It was not continuous, nor
were the same men involved all the time. But this cave-
system presented such problems, such dangers, that a
succession of attempts had to be made upon it, each
expedition having learned much from those that went
before; it was a long-drawn-out campaign waged with
immense courage and pertinacity, in which triumph and
tragedy were closely mingled.

The first step was to reinforce the entrance by cementing
the loose rocks. Where possible, rocks were removed bodily;
otherwise they were braced with transverse joists and steel
bars. To the site, 4,000 feet up the mountain, a pedal-
operated winch was manhandled: a massive structure
of steel tubes on which was mounted a drum carrying
an enormous length of five-millimetre stranded-steel
cable. This was geared to a pair of reinforced cycle pedals
coupled to a pair of hand-turned pedals such as are used
in invalid-chairs: this meant that the operator, mounted
on a saddle, could alternate between using feet and hands,
or use both together at need. The apparatus was mounted
on a framework securely anchored at the entrance to the
shaft. The reason for introducing a winch was that preliminary investigation had revealed that the initial drop,
almost completely vertical, was no less than 1,100 feet!

To climb down, let alone up, a shaft that length, even
on a flexible ladder, would be impossible. True there were

two ledges, the first at about 400 feet down, the second at about 700 feet, on to which a climber might with luck be able to swing himself and temporarily rest; but even at that the task would be beyond the strength and stamina of any pot-holer, however keen. So, strong harness had been designed; the harness was to be attached to a steel hook after it had been fitted securely on the pot-holer, and he would then be lowered, like a sack of potatoes, to the base of the first shaft. He would have a lifeline and a telephone line so that he could report back on what he found 1,100 feet down.

Much attention had been paid to detail. For example, since stranded cable always produces 'spin', the hook was swivelled: thus (it was hoped) the man would descend without spinning, whatever the cable did; and so he would be spared the risk of dizziness and the greater danger of being slung against a projecting rock during his descent and perhaps knocked unconscious: an eventuality he could not guard against if he had been overcome with dizziness.

Two of the most experienced pot-holers elected to be the first men down: Marcel Loubens and Henri Tazieff. Loubens went first. Having strapped on his harness and attached his throat-microphone to the telephone-cable, the other end of which was attached to head-phones worn permanently by one or other of the members at the operational base at the entrance to the shaft, he slipped over the lip of the shaft—into the unknown. From that point onwards he was at the mercy of a man in a saddle whose legs and arms had to turn the winding drum. He suggested to him that it might be a good idea to turn pretty slowly.

The 1,100-foot descent took almost two hours. During that descent Loubens made some discoveries about the harness: the steady pull on it caused the straps to tighten about him so that it became a strait-jacket; his chest was compressed until breathing became an agony; his stomach-muscles were strained, his shoulders pulled out of true. By the end of the two hours, when his cramped and half-frozen feet made contact with the base of the shaft, he was incapable of standing and collapsed in a heap on the loose rocks piled up all over the place. He had just the strength to wrench off his harness and begin to recover his breath. Then he signalled for the cable to be wound in so that his companion could join him.

It was not a comfortable spot in which to await him. The rock floor rather resembled a staircase: a steep one, with a falling gradient of about 1 in 2—say thirty degrees. It seemed to consist of enormous, irregular boulders between and under which there flowed a stream of icy-cold water. It was—though he did not know it at the time—to constitute the advance operational base for exploration that at times seemed likely never to come to an end. And also the scene of tragedy.

In due course Tazieff joined Loubens down below, bringing with him ultra-powerful lighting equipment. With this they established the fact that this cavern into which the shaft had dropped them was so gigantic that it could with ease have contained the great cathedral of Notre Dame de Paris! In honour of the intelligent bird-watcher-ornithologist to whom they owed this discovery they promptly named it: Lépineux Cave.

They had brought down with them 'fortified' biscuits and 'vitaminized' chocolate paste, sufficient to last them for some time. So when they had recovered from the discomfort of their descent they telephoned back to operational base that they were setting off on the second stage of exploration and would report again in twelve hours' time. Until then, 'not to worry'!

Working their way down the precipitous 'floor-staircase' of Lépineux Cave they found that the boulders in time gave place to pebbles, gravel and grit; the water by then had spread out and was flowing shallow and wide; but it came narrow again as it poured in through an opening in the rock at the further end of the gigantic cavern, an opening best described as a bottle-neck of rock. The two men flashed their lamps through it. By their combined beams they saw a wilderness of jumbled loose rock more or less filling the tunnel from side to side and from floor to roof. Through it, water ran steadily, to vanish over a lip of rock. They moved into the entrance, and pitched stones ahead of them, hoping to discover from their sound whether it was a cavern or a shaft. But they learned nothing by this method. Loubens decided to investigate for himself.

A length of rope was anchored to a boulder, and then Loubens thrust his legs through, gripped the rope tightly and began to work himself backwards and downwards with the pressure of his elbows. From that moment onwards his sole contact with his companion was the thin rope; and with the outside world, the telephone-cable point at the foot of the 1,100-foot shaft. He came at length to a platform which seemed safe enough, though there were many dangerously balanced boulders on it. He called to Tazieff to join him, and Tazieff lowered to him a flexible stranded-steel ladder before following him down.

H

Below was a further drop, much steeper: in fact, a shaft. They anchored the ladder and once again Loubens disappeared over the edge, leaving his companion on guard so that if he got into trouble he could either assist him or go back for help. The ladder was necessary because of the steepness of the shaft, whose bottom they had only been able to guess at. Tazieff watched the snap-link that held it to the anchor on the platform, judging Loubens's progress by the movements of the taut stranded steel.

He watched it for two hours: hours that, as is always the case deep down here, passed with dragging footsteps. Loubens was out of sight. Though he called back to him up the shaft, the reverberations were such that Tazieff could not understand what he was saying. And he had instructions not to leave the anchor and climb down—'just in case'.

At long last, the lamp on Loubens's helmet became visible, jogging about in the darkness far down the shaft. The ladder began to vibrate. Tazieff watched the snap-link, shining his torch down the shaft to encourage his companion as he laboriously climbed up to him. '*Eh bien?*' he called out, anxious to hear what Loubens had discovered.

The other man struggled over the lip of the shaft and lay on the platform, breathless and exhausted from the sheer physical effort of climbing that interminable ladder. But at last he was able to report. The deep shaft had brought him down into a second cavern, a cavern so colossal that it dwarfed even the vast Lépineux Cave. One thousand six hundred feet long, he had reckoned it, after a careful survey; 1,000 feet from side to side; and at least 300 feet high, to judge by the echoes, for his torch would not penetrate the darkness beneath the roof!

They were at once filled with elation; and sorry that they could not go any further: but they had used up all the rope and flexible laddering they had been able to bring with them down that first shaft. A greater number of men, more amply equipped, would have to undertake the next stage. Slowly, tired now that the excitement was over, they worked their way back up the shaft, through the long, rock-filled, sloping tunnel, across the rock-strewn floor of the Lépineux Cave to the foot of the shaft. Tazieff glanced at his watch: it was just twelve hours since they had descended; within a few minutes of the time they had promised to renew contact with their operational base. Loubens picked up the telephone; the man on the winch got busy, and first one and then the other began the long ascent of the 1,100-foot shaft to the surface—a journey slower by far even than the descent had been, for a man's dead-weight had to be hoisted up that shaft on the end of a stranded-steel cable by the power of another man's turning legs and arms.

Two points in Loubens's report were of prime significance. The first, that he had descended to no less than 1,650 feet—deeper than any man had been known to descend in France before; the second, that there was a strong flow of good water even at that great depth. The importance of this second point was that the region was one in which it was hoped to discover an extra source of water for a planned hydro-electric undertaking. It now looked, from Loubens's report, as though a new supply existed, and could be tapped. The French National Centre of Scientific Research undertook to sponsor further investigation, with this in mind.

One or two members of the team had had to leave

because their occupations made it impossible for them to spend as long in and around the Gouffre Pierre Saint-Martin as was obviously going to be necessary. But their places were taken by others. In fact, the original twelve became thirteen. No one apparently noticed that the total was now an 'unlucky' number; but it was not long before it was proved that there was after all something in that superstition!

More money was now put at the team's disposal. Jean Janssens, who had done the bulk of the winch operating—and reckoned he had done the equivalent of a hundred miles of hard pedalling, and *all uphill*!—was glad to find that a power-operated winch was to replace the one on which he had worked so hard. More and more rope, rope laddering, stranded-steel cables and tackle of many kinds was bought and carried up to the cave mouth.

The operational base camp took on new dimensions. Under canvas, in sheds, materials and gear and provisions accumulated. More and more ropes, rope ladders, flexible steel ladders, stiffened ladders for bridging; inflatable rubber canoes, diving-suits, powerful lamps whose focus could be varied for different purposes. And provisions: sardines, sides of bacon, legs and shoulders of ham, whole cheeses, bottles of red and white wine, chests of coffee beans, stacks of tins of condensed milk, noodles, onions, eggs, biscuits—nothing that a team of thirteen hungry and thirsty Frenchmen could possibly want to eat or drink was overlooked. This was a campaign, the end of which might be far away; campaigners must feed well if they are to succeed!

Once again, the experienced Marcel Loubens made the descent first. He carried with him powerful flood-lighting equipment which he had undertaken to establish at the base of the shaft so that Tazieff, who was to descend next, and who was an expert photographer, could take photographs at intervals in the shaft for record purposes. Once at the bottom, he signalled back that he was ready to receive him.

Tazieff, who tended to feel the cold, and knew that his job of photographing meant keeping reasonably warm, wrapped himself up in thick woollen underclothing, a woollen shirt, a heavy sweater, thick trousers and underpants, and an overall, topping the lot with heavy waterproofs, and a steel helmet! He was fitted into his harness, the ring on his harness snapped into the swivel hook on the steel cable, and prepared to descend. And it was on this descent that the new and much-prized power-operated winch showed the first signs of 'temperament'.

Tazieff was not fifty feet down the 1,100-foot shaft when the drum jammed and refused to turn any more. He was left there suspended in mid-air in his tight harness; which was bad enough. But something was wrong, too, with the swivel: perhaps his weight, with all that additional clothing, was too much for it! At any rate, it ceased to function. As a result of which the unhappy man, already half-suffocated by his harness, revolved a dozen times or so clockwise, then 'unwound' a dozen times or so, and then began the procedure all over again. That is one of the disadvantages of any stranded cable; but of course no other type of cable would have been at once light enough and strong enough for the job it had to do.

Tazieff was just beginning to wonder whether he would survive the appalling giddiness of the motion, when the drum slipped, and he dropped a considerable distance, only to be pulled up short as the drum jammed again, and of course practically suffocated by the sudden additional constriction of his harness. Every last ounce of breath was driven from his lungs and the effort to refill them was almost more than he could manage. He tried to call back up the shaft to ask when his torture would come to an end, but had not the breath to spare. Then there was another drop, another violent jerk; he began to ask himself what would become of him if the next sudden drop did *not* end with a jerk at all, but allowed him to continue down the full 1,100 feet of the shaft. He already knew the answer; and it was not a pleasant one.

Eventually, however, the drum was freed and he was lowered to Loubens, whose first task was to try to restore the circulation in Tazieff's legs and arms and to revive him from the flask of brandy he always carried for use in emergency. Then they set to work to put up a tent and inflate the air-mattresses that had been lowered in advance of them; for this was to be an advanced operational base. It was not a pleasant spot. The 'floor' was little more than a flight of steep, rough boulder steps, and water flowed continuously down them so that it was hard to find a safe and dry spot for the camp.

They were duly joined by others, with more equipment, including supplies of fluorescein, which they were to release into the water at various points in an attempt to ascertain its direction, rate of flow and quantity, and the rifts in the mountainside lower down where it emerged could therefore be piped and tapped. This fluorescein was a very fine powder that looked vermilion in artificial light but produced a brilliant emerald colour, even when only a few parts of it were introduced into a considerable quantity of water. Officials in the valley and at strategic spots on the lower slopes of the mountain were continually on duty to report results to the authorities.

The team operating from the advanced base at the foot of the shaft, in the vast Lépineux Cave, worked at their surveying and exploration for five days on end. They shifted tons of rubble, laid bare unsuspected fissures in the rock walls, diverted streams, checked their flow and charted their movements. At the end of the fifth day Loubens decided to return to the top of the 1,100-foot shaft for consultation; also to allow someone else to take his place down below while he took a turn at the much less interesting routine work on the winch and telephone and in the store-room.

He donned his harness, and attached to it some of the equipment for which they had no further need down below. He checked the swivel hook on the steel cable. It had already been checked, after Tazieff's unhappy experience, and seemed now to be working all right again. To make doubly sure, Loubens greased its bearings once more, and then hooked his harness on to it by its spring-loaded clip. Then the signal was given to the winch operator to hoist away, and Loubens prepared for the long, tedious and most uncomfortable lift up the shaft: no one had found a method of adjusting the harness so that it did not turn into a strait-jacket after a very short period, the members of the team just had to bear it—and grin if they could!

He had been lifted about fifty feet up the shaft from the base in Lépineux Cave when once again the drum jammed. A message was telephoned down the shaft to the advance base that a piece of cable had crossed on the

drum but would soon be released. Tazieff shouted the
good news up the shaft to the man dangling fifty feet
above his head. Loubens grunted his satisfaction, but did
not count on anything: he knew better, by now! The few
minutes became a quarter of an hour, half an hour, an
hour; and still he dangled on the cable, turning very
slowly a dozen or so times one way, and then a dozen
times the other way: that swivel still did not function as it
was supposed to do. He called down to Tazieff to
telephone up to the winch man suggesting that he should
be lowered, the fault corrected and then start the ascent
all over again. The reply was that the drum would not
revolve in either direction; he must be patient. Patient!
Loubens smiled grimly, but made no comment. It might
be a good thing, he thought, to give that winch man a
spell on the end of this infernal cable: he could then
practise what he now preached!

At long last the message came down the telephone that
the winch was freed: stand by, Marcel Loubens! Tazieff
called the good news up to his friend, who just managed to
wave a stiff arm in acknowledgment. Then the drum
began to turn, and the watchers down below saw
Loubens's dangling body begin to rise up the centre of the
shaft. He had a lamp attached to his harness, and as he
turned and turned, it revolved round the shaft like a
miniature lighthouse beam, illuminating the jutting rocks
that made the shaft such an uncomfortable one to ascend
and descend.

'A hundred feet!' Tazieff said to his companions watching with him in the Lépineux Cave. 'How glad he will be
when——'

He broke off short. Suddenly, faster than it takes to tell

it, Loubens's dangling, swivelling body jerked downwards. The lamp on his harness flashed on the shaft wall, descending at a speed far greater, they all knew, than the winch could possibly turn—if it was under control. And before any of them had fully taken in the horror of what was happening, they heard an agonized cry, followed immediately afterwards by the terrible thud of a body smashing down on the boulders at their very feet. It leapt and bounced from rock to rock on that steeply sloping floor; and eventually came to rest spread-eagled over two rocks, sagging horribly between them, hideously distorted. There followed silence: utter and complete silence.

Tazieff immediately ran to him, leaping like a chamois over the tumbled boulders. He dropped to his knees. Blood was flowing from Loubens's mouth and nose— proof of severe internal injury. From the contorted limbs it looked as though his spine and pelvis must be broken. If his spinal cord was broken too, then Loubens must be dead already.

They stood round him, the other members of the team down there, in despair, while Tazieff, his ear close to his friend's mouth, strove to catch any sign of breathing. None of them had any medical knowledge. André Mairey, the doctor attached to the expedition, was at the surface, 1,100 feet above their heads. The only means of access was a stranded-steel cable which, as Tazieff had already realized, had snapped off at the swivel. One of the others scrambled back up the rock steps to the telephone. Mercifully that cable had not been affected by Loubens's fall. He called for the doctor, to obtain instructions as to what to do next. The man at the winch, of course, already knew that the cable had failed.

What to do with Loubens: that was the immediate problem. To leave him where he lay meant that if, as so often happened, some rock was dislodged and fell, it might fall on him; to move him—always a dangerous thing to do without medical supervision, and when the full details of a victim's injuries were not known—might equally be fatal. Tazieff decided it was the lesser of the two risks. With infinite caution, trying not to alter in any way the position or angle of his legs or arms, they contrived to insert a piece of canvas beneath him. On this improvised stretcher they carried him, with infinite care, till he was clear of the base of the shaft. It took them half an hour to move him no more than twenty yards.

Miraculously, Loubens was still breathing—if it could be called breathing: blood was oozing from the corner of his mouth, frothing and bubbling as it came. His upper jaw was unmistakably fractured, and badly; one leg was certainly broken, and probably the other as well; almost certainly, too, the spine and pelvis: Loubens was a shattered man.

Down there in the advanced operations camp they watched over him. There was nothing they could do for him; only Dr Mairey could do anything. And until a new cable had been mounted, and tested, he could not even be lowered; and when that was possible, it still needed an hour or two for the descent.

The vigil seemed unending. It was momentarily relieved for them when to their amazement they saw Marcel Loubens move an arm slowly towards his hip: a mute statement that it was paining him badly. They tried to wedge soft material beneath the hip to ease it, but knew it could make little difference to him. From time to time a faint groan came from between his lips. They prayed for the arrival of the doctor; but the winch had jammed again, and until the cable could be hauled in, checked, fitted with a new swivel, and made ready for lowering, the doctor could not come.

At last the cable was seen to move: it began snaking away from the foot of the shaft, up into the darkness. The watchers renewed their hope that all soon would be well. One of them went to the telephone to ask what the prospects were. And as he picked up the receiver—the line went dead! Somewhere in that 1,100 feet of cable a fault had developed. The watchers were now completely cut off from help from up above.

There began the next stage in their vigil down below: a stage infinitely more exacting than the earlier stages, for now they had no chance of receiving comfort from those overhead, they could make no more reports; they were completely alone. They were alone for no less than fifteen hours, cut off from all contact with the others at the main base. It was impossible to believe that it should take so long to wind in a cable, fit a new swivel and lower it—again. They were not to know that the drum was continuing to give trouble, the motor continuously failing. To have let Dr Mairey descend on an unreliable winch could well have meant a second tragedy.

Loubens's breathing became more laboured. The frothing blood that oozed from his lips was only a tiny trickle, but it meant that he must be losing what little strength remained to him. He groaned at intervals, showing signs of regaining consciousness, and those watching over him prayed that he would not do so, as then he would be conscious of the pain of his shattered limbs, for which they could do nothing at all.

By now they themselves were exhausted with the strain of watching, their desperate fears for their dying comrade. They divided into two watches, and one tried to snatch a little sleep while the other watch stood by the telephone-line and watched for the cable, praying for some sign from up above.

At eight o'clock in the morning—*twenty* hours after Loubens had fallen down the shaft—a voice came down the telephone-line, which had at last been repaired, to say that the winch was now in order, a new cable wound on to it and Dr Mairey was about to descend the shaft. They counted not merely the minutes but the seconds till he arrived, travelling down that shaft at a speed which was dangerous, so anxious was he to arrive in time.

He whipped off his harness, and dropped to Loubens's side, taking the place which had been occupied by Tazieff almost without a break for twenty hours. With practised fingers he made his diagnosis. The skull, in spite of the spun-glass helmet, was fractured; the spinal column, also, was fractured. There were other fractures, only just less serious. Of the pelvis he could not yet be certain, though he feared so. André Mairey gave Loubens injections in order that he should not recover consciousness whatever happened to him on the ascent. For one thing the doctor had known from the first: that he must be got to hospital without delay. Already a helicopter had been commissioned for transport.

Loubens was lifted with expert care and a stretcher slipped beneath him. He was padded with wedges of cotton-wool and down taken from the sleeping-bags, wrapped about with the inflatable mattresses, and strapped securely to the stretcher so that whatever angle it assumed during the long, slow ascent he would not be affected by it.

Meanwhile a great number of flexible and other ladders had been lowered down the shaft. Members of the team had to climb or descend these and station themselves at intervals so that when the stretcher came to them they could make sure that it did not turn or swing against the walls of the shaft and injure the unconscious man strapped to it. This in itself was a hazardous task, and one which would never even have been contemplated had it not been for the seriousness of the situation. The movement of the ladders, and the men stationed in the shaft, caused many stones to be dislodged. Dr Mairey, still working on the stretcher case, realized that any one of these might prove the final blow. He therefore fitted Loubens's helmet back on his head, and secured it with bands of adhesive tape in such a way that it would remain in position and prevent his head from being jerked about during the ascent. The last thing he did was to give him a blood transfusion to replace some at least of the blood he had so obviously lost since his fall.

And at that very moment a deep, stuttering, choking groan came from the man on the stretcher. There was a rattle in his throat, faint at first, then increasing in volume, and then fading away entirely. Dr Mairey was instantly at his side. He flashed his torch on him. The watchers saw a grave look pass over his face, followed by a look of utter defeat. Then he turned to the others. Slowly he shook his head. They knew, without his speaking, what that meant: their fellow pot-holer, the indomitable Marcel Loubens, who had seemed to bear a charmed life, for he had come near to death so often in the past in other descents, had died.

Tazieff closed Loubens's eyelids. The torches were switched off. The little group stood in silence round the stretcher as it rested there among them, their heads bent in prayer. All their efforts had failed. It was thirty-six hours since Loubens had fallen. For the whole of that time they had watched over him, seeking what small things they could do to ease him. For the last twelve hours they had had Dr Mairey with them, using all his skill and knowledge to save his life. Now they were standing in the Lépineux Cave, having failed in what they had tried so hard, so loyally, to do.

After long discussion all idea of raising Loubens's body to the surface was abandoned: the winch had failed too often already; if it failed once again it would seem like desecration. He should be buried here, at the site of the advanced operational camp from which he had so expertly directed the underground survey. And the remote cavern which he, Marcel Loubens, had been the first to enter and explore, should be named after him: the Loubens Cave. There were one or two members who thought it would be fitting that he should be transferred to that cave and buried there; but Tazieff, who had assisted him through that series of passages and vertical shafts, knew better; it would be impossible to manhandle a body on a stretcher to that remote cavern in the deepest and most inaccessible part of the Gouffre Pierre Saint-Martin. The idea was abandoned.

They set about the sad task of finding a suitable spot for a grave in the Lépineux Cave. Boulders were removed and a hollow found in the floor, clear of the watercourse. Into it, reverently, they lowered Loubens's body,

still in his padded canvas shroud and wearing the
battered helmet. As they looked down upon him in
the cavity they had excavated he seemed to them to
resemble some medieval knight in full armour. Like those
old knights, he had a stone for a pillow and his feet were
crossed on another stone.

. Over him they heaped a great cairn of stones. At the
end of the cairn they erected a cross, painted in luminous
paint on a slab of black limestone that had two bands of
white slanting across it. One of their number, an Italian
named Beppo Occhialini, inscribed on a slab of rock with
the flame of an acetylene lamp:

HERE

MARCEL LOUBENS

PASSED THE LAST DAYS OF HIS GALLANT LIFE

And then they turned away, to begin the long and
wearisome ascent of the 1,100-foot shaft. Each man,
before beginning the ascent—Henri Tazieff, Loubens's
close friend and supporter, Dr André Mairey, who had
fought so hard to save his life, the tough Janssens, who
had operated the original pedal winch in the earlier
expedition, Laisse and Labeyrie, Max Cosyns, Robert
Levi and the Italian, Beppo Occhialini—turned to have
one last look over his shoulder at what he was leaving
behind him. Weirdly in the darkness the cross they had
erected on the cairn glimmered with its luminous paint—
paint that had been designed for use in marking out the
route in dark corners and that they had never expected
to have to put to such a tragic use.

*   *   *   *   *

The story of the probing of the notorious Gouffre Pierre Saint-Martin is a long one; but then the operation itself was an extended one. Extended, and eventful too: and always accompanied by major or minor disaster.

Loubens had reported that at 1,650 feet, the ultimate point that he was able to reach, there was still a flow of water, but he could see no way of pursuing and channelling it further. For the time being, because of the tragedy of his death, no further exploration was undertaken. But a year later a new expedition was organized. It had a twofold aim: to probe yet further than Loubens had probed; and to recover his body and bring it to the surface so that it could be buried near his family. Among the members of this expedition was Dr André Mairey.

The team approached the cave with some apprehension. It had already killed once; it might have further tragedy to inflict. And in fact it was not long before it began running true to form. Dr Mairey was the next casualty. He fell on a treacherous length of sloping rock and injured his arm; not very badly, but badly enough to handicap him severely for the remainder of the operation.

So, suspicion grew that there was some living spirit of malevolent attitude inhabiting the Gouffre Pierre Saint-Martin, determined to thwart all attempts to probe its mysteries. But the suspicion did not prevent the team from continuing operations.

Their courage and persistence were rewarded. They found another exit from the remote Loubens Cave: a difficult tunnel, succeeded by a dangerous shaft, and then a series of tunnels and shafts, each narrower and more tortuous than the last, ending in a final subterranean chamber that proved, when altimeters and other instru-

ments had been compared and checked, to be no less than
2,395 feet below ground! This was an absolute and all-
time record for a pot-hole system: a depth a good deal
greater than anything hitherto known.

The team, exhausted by the arduousness of their exploration, but at the same time triumphant over their success,
wearily climbed back up and through the series of shafts
and tunnels, crawls, chambers and squeezes, until they
came to the vast Lépineux Cave. By the time they reached
their advanced operational base they were so exhausted
that they were tripping and falling and had to cling to one
another for support. They came to the base of the main
shaft. One of their number reached for the telephone to
send up to the surface their great news. And at that very
moment the spirit of Gouffre Pierre Saint-Martin decided
that it had still a card to play. It struck again.

There was a sudden terrifying roar, and an avalanche
of stone and rubble, a landslide of rock, fell down the
vertical shaft. Not to the base of it but part way only. And
there it jammed tight, like an enormous cork of stone. So
tightly that it crushed the stranded-steel winch cable into
the rock wall and snapped through the telephone-line.
Now, between the men at the foot of the shaft and those
at the main base at the surface, there was no possibility
of contact; no possibility even of sending messages.

It was an appalling predicament in which they found
themselves. They were already exhausted from their
penetration to that record depth of 2,395 feet; the food
supplies were down to their lowest limit; their lamps were
no longer at full strength, and reserves of batteries and
carbide were almost completely used up; the temperature
in the Lépineux Cave was only a few degrees above

I

freezing-point; most of them had minor injuries—cuts, bad bruises and abrasions, twisted ankles, strained muscles; they were pretty well at the end of their powers of resistance.

There was nothing they could do to help themselves. The stone 'cork' might be a few feet thick, or many yards. It might, if they were rash enough to try to loosen it from below, disintegrate and smash down, killing the lot of them. All they could do was wait, cut their rations to the barest minimum and pray for rescue from above.

It came—in time. Somehow their companions overhead succeeded in prising loose the main slabs that were holding the bulk of the rocks fast in the shaft. The landslide continued to the bottom—fortunately without injuring any of those waiting below, who had had the good sense to re-pitch their tents well away from the foot of the shaft. The 'staircase' of loose rock that made the so-called floor of the Lépineux Cave was now covered with a great apron of scree. Over this the exhausted, half-frozen men, starved, and many of them suffering greatly from exposure, had to be helped to the base of the shaft by those who had come down to rescue them, and then be hoisted one at a time up the sheer 1,100 feet of shaft to the surface; and as they were hoisted up they knew that where one landslide had taken place, another might well follow it. It was a miracle that there were no deaths in that stage of the campaign.

You might think that the experience of 1953 would have been sufficient to choke-off any further exploration. But though the problem of the water supply had been solved, and the final depth of the Gouffre Pierre Saint-Martin established, the other objective—the recovery of

Marcel Loubens's body—had not been achieved. In 1954 another, and final, stage in this protracted campaign began.

A specially designed aluminium-alloy coffin, stream-lined so as to offer the least possible resistance, had been prepared, and was carried to the main operational base near that frontier stone 6,000 feet up on the Franco-Spanish Pyrenees. The members of this expedition had sworn not to return without Marcel Loubens's body. They took, therefore, the most meticulous precautions against anything going wrong.

A new, stronger, stranded-steel cable was wound on to the drum of the winch, which itself had been checked over by engineers; drum and cable and gear were lavishly greased. A series of ladders, each tested inch by inch in advance, was lowered down the side of the shaft, each one locked securely to the one above and below it, and each one braced to the solid rock by strong pitons. The reason for this elaborate laddering was this: it had been decided that the coffin, when it began its ascent, must be accompanied the whole way by a member of the expedition, who would watch it, check its sway if it developed, protect it from collision with the shaft sides. José Bidegain volunteered for this most exacting task.

And it certainly was an exacting task. José Bidegain knew well what it would entail, for he had been a member of the 1953 expedition which had so nearly involved the deaths of all who were down below when the landslide blocked the 1,100-foot shaft. He faced the ordeal of climbing step by step from base to summit alongside the coffin. No one could relieve him, for the ladders could hardly be expected to take two men's weight.

The cable was lowered. Loubens's body was removed from beneath the great cairn of stones heaped over it by his companions, and carefully inserted into the aluminium-alloy coffin. This was then securely attached to a snap-link on the end of the cable. There was no need, this time, to use a swivel-hook, for it would not matter if it revolved as it ascended the shaft. Indeed it might be a good thing if it did; for any stone that might fall from above would then strike it only a glancing blow and be thrown clear.

Rung by rung, José Bidegain began the interminable climb: 1,100 feet in slow motion, clinging to thin ladder rails, his feet on thin ladder rungs, one hand always ready to make some adjustment to the coffin's position as it was hoisted up the shaft alongside him. It was a prospect to daunt anyone. The strain on his arms and legs increased with every fifty feet he climbed. It was a sheer lift the whole way, gravity dragging him downwards against the flexing of his arm and thigh muscles; and at any moment a stone might well drop on to his head or shoulder and by its impact knock him off his ladder, to fall to the base of the shaft and die as Marcel Loubens had died.

Above him, their lamps focused downwards on him as he climbed, the watchers held their breath, powerless to do more than encourage him with their words from time to time when he came within hearing distance. He came to within perhaps a dozen yards or so. Now they could see his knuckles, gleaming white as bone as he gripped the ladder rails. His face, half-upturned to them, was as white as death with the strain. The muscles of his neck stood out like knotted cords.

And then, suddenly, it became apparent to them that even a dozen yards was more than he was going to be able to manage: the last thirty or forty feet out of 1,100. He came to a standstill, clinging to his ladder with both hands, his head swaying from side to side. At any instant, they could see, he must let go, and fall to his death.

One man acted. Taking the risk of putting additional weight on a ladder, he lowered himself over the edge of the shaft. Someone dropped a noose of rope round him. Someone else called to Bidegain to hang on: help was at hand.

Somehow—he was never able to explain how he achieved the acrobatic feat—the man descended the narrow ladder and succeeded in embracing Bidegain with his body and arms so that he could not now fall even if he let go entirely. If he did fall—then it would be because the ladder had broken away from the pitons; and that would mean two deaths instead of one.

Miraculously, the ladder held. Rung by rung the two men climbed to the surface, a dozen yards feeling like twelve hundred. Willing hands hauled them over the lip of the shaft, to safety. Bidegain received instant medical attention from the expedition doctor; his rescuer, the strain once over, turned to assist in detaching the coffin from the cable which had by then hauled it to the surface. Loubens was back among his old companions once again!

And so the saga of the notorious killer cave, the Gouffre Pierre Saint-Martin, ended. Its ultimate depth, at 2,395 feet, had been plumbed; the problem of the distribution of the vital water-supplies had been solved; the body of the man who had been the prime mover in the explorations had been brought to the surface at long last. The spirit of the Gouffre Pierre Saint-Martin had played its last desperate card—and lost.

EIGHT: THE CHALLENGE OF GAPING GHYLL

THE English Pennines consist largely of gritstone and limestone, with a thin covering of turf on which sheep can graze, or a thick covering of moorland peat where grouse breed and other wild birds may sometimes be seen: barren, forbidding, inhospitable acres over which the experienced rambler sometimes takes his exercise and pleasure but which the amateur or faint-hearted is wise to avoid. Mists, great winds, driving rain are frequent there; even experienced walkers, familiar with the country, have been lost there in bad weather and have been known to die of exhaustion and exposure. The three summits, Ingleborough, Great Whernside and Pen-y-Ghent, dominate this lonely expanse of high and empty ground; strange outcrops of white rock, curiously weathered and pitted, break the surface; cavities with strange names—such as 'Butter-Tubs'—excite the curiosity of those who venture into the region; legends and folk-tales, rumours and superstitions, have grown up and been part of the lives of men and women and children whose ancestors have always lived within sight of these moors, within sound of the often frightening moorland 'music' produced by wind sighing over them, eroding the gritstone masses and, in winter-time, whipping the snow into great banks that completely alter the whole face of the moorland.

Shepherds rounding up their hardy moorland sheep at sheep-shearing and lambing time bring back to their cottages stories of fearsome sounds that cannot possibly be, they say, anything but supernatural—and therefore evil. Great cavities appear suddenly at their feet, they say; and from them there issue horrific cries, as of creatures imprisoned deep down here and striving to escape. Some of these cavities in the moorland, they will swear to their listeners, 'were not there last time we went by'! They may have been courageous enough to linger and throw a piece of rock down into the darkness. 'But those pits are bottomless!' Such a pit is Gaping Ghyll.

Gaping Ghyll is to be found exactly seven miles north-west of Settle, in the West Riding of Yorkshire. Hardly more than a mile further to the north-west is the great mass of Ingleborough, rising to 2,373 feet; beyond is Black Shiver Moss; to the north is the famous Alum Pot Hole; to the south of it, Clapham Beck and Ingleborough Cave. All round it are 'mosses'—the name often given to great areas of deep and dangerous bogland; and 'forces'— the name often given to the cataracts that pour over the gritstone and limestone formations into deep, dark pools. It is a dramatic and spectacular landscape even in bright sunshine; in bad weather, or even beneath a cloud-laden sky, it is forbidding indeed. The drivers of the pack-horse trains who travelled the tracks across these almost trackless moors made haste to be off them, and down in the valleys, before darkness fell. There was no end to the tales they told about Gaping Ghyll.

*   *   *   *   *

Not everyone listened to such tales and accepted them, however. Among those who doubted was a Yorkshireman named John Birkbeck, who in 1872 became exasperated by the way in which his fellow-townsmen of Settle comfortably believed all the yarns that came their way. He decided that the only way to persuade them of their folly was to go and see for himself, and then report back to them.

One day, therefore, he set off across the moor to see what he could find out. He took with him a great length of stout twine, which he had previously knotted at fifty-foot intervals, and a five-pound weight attached to the end of it. Having arrived at the mouth of the pot-hole, he prepared to find out whether or no it was 'bottomless', as everybody but himself now firmly believed. Being a prudent man, he first anchored himself to a heavy boulder close to the opening in the ground, so that if in his excitement he were to tip forward as he lowered his weighted twine there would be no risk of his falling down after it.

One . . . two . . . three . . . four . . . five . . . six . . . seven: the knots ran out through his hands; and at the seventh knot the weight came off the twine and he knew he had 'touched bottom'. Three hundred and fifty feet: so much for those pack-horse drivers' and others' yarns! To make absolutely sure, he hauled in his weighted twine, counting the knots as he did so, and then lowered it a second time. And again the weight came off the twine at the seventh knot. There was no doubt about it: the depth of this hole known as Gaping Ghyll was 350 feet, neither more nor less!

He noticed, however, that the twine was soaked

through. It did not surprise him, for there is a small beck, marked on the map as Fell Beck, which is fed from various tiny streamlets off Ingleborough and Simon Fell and runs due south down their slopes, to tumble into Gaping Ghyll. The twine, therefore, had been made wet as the water splashed against it; and of course there might well be a lake at the bottom of the shaft, for the water would naturally accumulate. Birkbeck decided he would go down and have a look for himself. This was an extremely brave—some might say foolhardy—thing to do, for in those days the sport of pot-holing had not been thought of in Britain.

The main problem, of course, was the stream of water pitching down into the pot-hole. Birkbeck solved the problem in an ingenious fashion. He hired a number of labourers and brought them up on to the moor, complete with their picks and shovels. They were instructed to dig a 1,000-yard channel in the peat, slanting towards a neighbouring ravine. Then the beck was to have a dam thrown across it so that its waters would be diverted into the new channel: it was as simple as that!

The scheme worked. Very soon there was hardly more than a trickle of water running in the old channel, that led to the mouth of the well-named Gaping Ghyll. John Birkbeck had had sent up on to the moor some lengths of good stout rope and also an improvised rope-ladder. He anchored the ends of these to the massive boulder he had used for his first attempt to plumb the depths with a length of weighted twine. Then, having made sure that the knots were sound and the boulder immovable, he courageously lowered himself over the edge of the shaft.

The length of his ropes, and the rope-ladder, was almost 200 feet: not sufficient, as he well knew, to reach the bottom; but enough, he hoped, to enable him to gather some idea of the condition of the shaft for rather more than half its depth. Luck was with him. At about 190 feet he found himself on a substantial ledge of rock that felt solid beneath his feet as he gingerly took first one and then the other off his rope-ladder. He stood there trying, with his very ineffective oil-lamp that he had slung on his belt, to peer over the edge and see what the second half of the shaft was like. But he could see only a few yards—roughly to the end of his ropes and ladder. For a moment or two he considered calling up to the men waiting for him to throw down the ropes so that he could continue his journey; but he had the good sense to realize that if they did this he would have no way of returning to the surface! Besides, he was already soaked to the skin, for though the main flow of water had been diverted there was still a good deal spurting out from cracks in the rock. He took the wiser decision and climbed back to safety.

Curiously enough, he made no more descents. He had satisfied himself as to the depth of the allegedly bottomless hole; and the fact that he had descended almost 200 feet into it, and returned without anything more unpleasant happening to him than a soaking from cold moorland water, proved the absurdity of the pack-horse drivers' yarns. He rested on his laurels; some of his friends accepted his statement about the pot-hole; and the simple pack-horse drivers, the shepherds and the local folk went on telling one another the stories they had always told, while the wind whistled outside the thick stone walls of their snug cottages and farms to remind them how much safer they were indoors than out! Gaping Ghyll's challenge had been taken up; and then dropped.

More than twenty years later, however, a Frenchman named Edouard-Alfred Martel, one of the first men to take up pot-holing scientifically, heard about the challenge of Gaping Ghyll, bought a ticket for Britain, made his way north to Settle and had a look round the moors that lay between that small town and the mass of Ingleborough. He was lucky enough to run into one of the men who had helped dig the new channel to divert Fell Beck, and he was impressed by the originality of the scheme. He hired some more men and supervised the digging out of the channel where it had caved in, had it lengthened considerably, had the dam reinforced and then waited patiently until the original watercourse dried up.

He had had more experience of these things than Birkbeck, and knew that though a watercourse might appear dry there would still be water beneath it, seeping down for scores, even for hundreds, of feet: there was little anyone could tell Edouard-Alfred Martel about the peculiarities of limestone! So he waited longer than the Yorkshireman had done; meanwhile collecting and assembling rope, flexible ladders and a number of stout oaken posts, together with a heavy wooden maul for driving them in. He was in no great hurry; it was his policy to prepare every move in detail, and well in advance; the policy had always paid off in the past and, he felt sure, would do so this time.

He had a number of these stout oak posts driven deep into the peat, as close as was safe to the edge of the shaft. To these, guy-ropes were attached, the other ends being attached to posts driven into the peat several yards away;

this produced a double-safe anchor. A beam was laid across the lip of the shaft, and a double rope prepared. To this a 300-foot flexible ladder was secured and then carefully lowered over the beam and down the shaft.

Martel gave instructions to the men he had engaged as guides, and then, having lit his lamp, proceeded to lower himself over the beam and on to the upper rungs of his ladder. Before he vanished down the shaft he checked the tension on the doubled rope that was attached to the anchor he had prepared. Then he descended. Moving fast but steadily he climbed down rung after rung until, at just short of the 200-foot mark, he came to the ledge on which John Birkbeck had stood and considered his next move. He tested it, and was satisfied. Then he called up for the ladder to be lowered on its doubled rope so that he could embark on the next stage of the descent.

It began snaking down towards him and he checked it by the fifty-foot marks he had made on it, lowering it past and beneath the ledge on which he stood and expertly checking each rung as it slipped through his practised hands. He sent up a second signal, and the ladder ceased to snake down towards him: the doubled rope had been made fast again to the anchor. He heaved strenuously at it, satisfied himself that the anchor was still firm and then proceeded to lower himself down the second half of the shaft, below the halfway shelf. In due course he touched bottom and found himself standing on a floor of rock, black sand and rounded pebbles. He surveyed the underground cavern in which he found himself, and then signalled that he was about to return.

Martel was a brisk worker. His descent had occupied only twenty-three minutes; his ascent of the 350-foot shaft occupied only five minutes longer! He was a man who would spend endless time in his preparations, leaving nothing to chance; then, satisfied that everything humanly possible had been done, he climbed. It was largely due to his inspiration that men like Norbert Casteret and other great French speleologists developed the craft of pot-holing to such a pitch. Oddly, though, Martel did not follow-up this descent. Satisfied that he, a Frenchman, had been the first to descend this English pot-hole, he returned to his native limestone and continued his subterranean explorations there.

Yorkshire's pride was mortally wounded! Only a month after E.-A. Martel had made the first successful descent, a group of Yorkshiremen under the leadership of a man named Calvert decided to take up this double challenge and make a complete and detailed survey of Gaping Ghyll. They were eight in all. They assembled a good deal of gear in the form of ropes, ladders and pulley-blocks and tackle and lugged it up on to the moor. Not wishing to be dependent on Martel's anchor they rigged a fresh anchor for themselves; and then Calvert, as leader, was lowered over the edge and down the shaft.

Unfortunately there had been heavy rain during that month, and though the beck was still being channelled off, there was water spurting out of crevices in the shaft wall and Calvert was soaked to the skin in no time. He stuck to his descent, however. And his determination was rewarded: on his return from surveying his quick eye spotted a rift in the rock wall of the shaft that gave him an idea. It showed a faint gleam of light, which suggested that it might be linked with another shaft not too far away.

This, if they could discover it, might offer them a better means of access to the cavern deep down the shaft.

They investigated. Yes, it was true: a lateral tunnel approximately five feet high and a yard wide ran for some fifteen feet, almost level, tapering as it did so, to give access to a second and hitherto unsuspected vertical shaft approximately six feet in diameter and—as they found by dropping stones down it—apparently 'bottomless'! They were so excited by the prospect of this 'back-door' mode of entry that they wanted to descend it right away. As leader, however, Calvert turned down the idea; judging by the heaviness of the rain they might expect to find deep water down there; it would be foolish to ruin their chances by being in too much of a hurry. They would have to wait, he told them.

In May the following year, however, he gathered his team and equipment together again. They had accumulated what for those early days of pot-holing was a very varied lot of gear. In addition to new ropes and ladders they had more elaborate pulley-blocks, leather and webbing harness, iron bars, wooden beams and much else. Above all, they pinned their faith to a massive winch designed to spare their muscles, which they manhandled up on to the rugged moorland.

They had brought a good deal of thought to bear on the problems, during the long winter evenings. One bright idea was to use lengths of rope which were alternately right-hand-twisted and left-hand: this, they thought, should spare them the discomfort of spinning in the air as they descended the shafts. To the end of this rope a bosun's-chair was attached by four strong cords. Calvert was strapped into this in readiness for the descent.

The precautions taken were elaborate. The main rope was wound round the winch. A secondary rope, strong enough to take a man's weight, was separately anchored, its upper end held by three members of the party and to be paid out cautiously so that it was always taut. If, as Calvert descended, anything went wrong either with the winch or with the main rope or the bosun's-chair, they would be able to hold him safely and bring him back to the surface.

Curiously enough, Calvert decided to use a pistol in order to communicate with those at the top of the shaft! He reckoned that a shot fired by him, however far down the shaft he might be, would certainly be heard by them. He was quite right in this. What he had failed to realize, however, was the effect of firing a pistol at the bottom of a shaft whose walls were solid rock. He did so once; and once only. The effect was shattering! The roar of the explosion reverberated all round him so violently that he himself was deafened, and for a long time afterwards feared that he would never recover his hearing. The pistol was abandoned for a less dangerous form of signalling.

He touched bottom at 350 feet, finding, to his surprise, water up to his knees. It was extremely cold, but did not seem to have much movement, for which he was thankful. He was about to climb out of the bosun's-chair and begin surveying the chamber to find out if there was anything beyond it when his lamp went out. He tried in vain to light it. Then, having failed, he signalled that he wished to be hoisted to the surface. He did not look forward to the return trip overmuch as the device of the left-hand-right-hand-twisted rope had not proved a success!

Next day he made a second descent. This time he took

with him an improvised field-telephone. Unfortunately during the descent the cable was damaged and when he touched bottom he found that he was cut off from communication with those above him. Again it seemed to him unwise to prospect any further since he had lost touch with the others, so he ascended once more in his uncomfortable spinning bosun's-chair. As he ascended, he succeeded in rescuing the telephone-cable and carrying it with him to the surface, where it was carefully repaired and made ready for use on his next descent. But this time it was the water that caused the trouble: it spurted into a junction-box and disconnected him from the party at the surface: it looked to Calvert as though he was doomed to fail.

Finally, however, he succeeded, and established a route down which other members of his team were able to follow him, Gray and Booth, his closest friends, among them. They assembled at the foot of the shaft and by the combined light of their lamps succeeded in surveying the cavern in which they now found themselves. It staggered them by its proportions. Though it was not comparable with the great caverns at the bottom of the French potholes yet to be discovered, it was immense: nearly 500 feet in length, they estimated; over 100 feet high and nearly 100 feet in width!

The floor had been worn into channels by the water, but when they stepped clear of the channels they were on dry rock. At its eastern end there was what looked like a great staircase of rubble slanting steeply upwards to a height of about seventy feet. This they began to climb. They were surprised to find, about a quarter of the way up, a quantity of wool and sheep-bones. The find suggested that in the winter months, and when the snow was melting on the moors, this vast cavern was filled with water to a depth of fifteen feet and more, and this represented 'high-water mark' at which the remains of sheep that had fallen down the 350-foot shaft were washed up and deposited.

They succeeded in climbing to the top of the seventy-foot rubble staircase, and found at the summit a narrow, horizontal slit. Shining their lamps into it they found that it ran inwards for some distance. In width it was little more than a yard at the most; in height it was hardly more than twelve inches. Moreover, there were short, blunted stalactites hanging down from the ceiling of the tunnel like giants' teeth. Short, blunt stalagmites pointed upwards to meet them: it resembled a whale's or shark's mouth, designed to keep intruders out or to devour them if they were foolhardy enough to try to enter it.

Nevertheless this is just what Calvert resolved to do. With his friend Gray in close support he thrust himself into the slit and squirmed his way forward like a lizard, breaking off the stalagmites and stalactites where this was possible, and sliding past them where they were too tough to break off. There was no turning back. They were determined to find out 'what lay ahead'—the basic urge of the pot-holer, wherever he may find himself.

Eventually they emerged from the squeeze into a passage, the first as it proved of a series of passages. Some of these were no larger than the one through which they had just forced their way; others were comparatively roomy; others again were quite literally impossible to enter: mere fissures in the solid limestone. They worked their way into a chamber in which they could stand upright and walk about; then to another chamber, much

K

larger, nearly as large, indeed, as the first one they had
entered at the foot of the main shaft. From what they
could see of it by the light of their two combined lamps
they were only now on the threshold of an absolute wilderness of passages and shafts and caverns. There were curious
rock ledges; there were substantial ridges at different
levels; there were formations such as they had never
dreamed of. And all this tempted further exploration.

Calvert realized—as so many pioneers have realized in
like conditions—that a successful exploration of such a
subterranean world demanded a larger party, with stage-
points linking the advance party with the base, and with
equipment even more ample than they had collected
already. He gave the order to return and set about organ-
izing an expedition on a bigger scale than anything
organized before. At that time he fondly believed that he
and his party would soon have plumbed the ultimate
mysteries of Gaping Ghyll: how little he knew!

The pot-holers returned. They brought ample equipment. They explored each passage, each shaft, in turn,
charted it and reported back to base. They wrote-off some
of the passages that had water in them—for they knew
nothing of Casteret's technique of 'forcing a siphon'; others
they wrote-off because they were just too tight to squeeze
through with the best will in the world; they checked water
levels, rate of flow and temperature, and duly recorded all
these data; they compiled a detailed map which revealed
(as they then thought) every nook and cranny of this
newly discovered world far down beneath the bleak
Yorkshire moorland; they had every reason to feel
satisfied with themselves when they returned up the
main shaft for the last time, with their exploration com-

plete: nothing like this had ever been attempted in Britain before.

But pot-holing is something which seems never to have a recognizable end: there is always, the pot-holer believes, something else just round the corner. And almost invariably he is right. It is certainly the case with Gaping Ghyll. For many years successive groups of pot-holers, large and small, have continued to explore it since Calvert, Gray and Booth and their party came up, satisfied that they had exhausted its possibilities. Several miles of entirely new tunnels and shafts have been successfully located and opened up—often as the result of most arduous and dangerous pioneer work by experts and the use of newly developed experimental techniques.

No pot-holer, however many hours he has spent in Gaping Ghyll, will agree that he has exhausted its possibilities. There are, he knows, many tunnels at present filled with water which, one day, he hopes he may be able to penetrate—either by skin-diving or by channelling-off the water as Birkbeck and Martel did at the surface and as the pot-holers in the Eisriesenwelt succeeded so notably in doing. He knows, too, that even the dry tunnels, some of them at any rate, can be suddenly and unexpectedly filled with water when heavy rain falls without warning on the moors many hundreds of feet overhead. It has happened before; and will happen again: it is an occupational hazard.

Quite recently, in fact, a party of expert pot-holers were deep down in one of the remoter caverns of the Gaping Ghyll system. There had been a long, dry spell, though the possibility of rain had been forecast. They were in a well-charted section of the cave-system—which was fortunate for them. For they heard, first to their surprise and then to their consternation, the sound of moving water where none had been till that moment. The leader of the party, a man who had spent some hundreds of hours down in Gaping Ghyll, gave the order to move, and to move fast. They did so, recognizing the urgency in his voice.

They made swiftly for the ladders by which they had descended the shaft leading to the cavern, only to find that the tunnel leading to those ladders was already cut off from them by fast-moving water. Their leader knew of an alternative route, and took it, moving now as fast as it was possible to move underground. He led them to a rock face that could—with a great effort—be scaled without the use of ladders and, with luck, take them up beyond the reach of the flood.

Shinning up that rock face as though the devil himself was after them, they came to a ridge and, by a superhuman effort, succeeded in clambering on to it. They were only just in time. Peering downwards, they saw black water swirling about at the foot of the rock. In the light of their lamps they saw that the water level was rising—and rising fast. One by one the handholds and toeholds by which they had scaled the rock were obliterated: there seemed no reason why the water should cease to rise till it reached their ledge.

They glanced anxiously upwards, and could see at once that there was no hope of further escape that way: the rock face above their ledge was smooth as glass, sheer, and quite devoid of even the smallest cracks by which they might hope to climb. Their fate—if the water continued to rise—seemed to be sealed.

Then Chance took a hand. In spite of the loneliness of

that stretch of moorland it happened that a fell-walker was crossing it and turned aside, in spite of the rain, to have a look at the entrance to Gaping Ghyll. To his astonishment, muffled, strangled cries for help came floating up the shaft: someone, obviously, was in distress. He waited just long enough to yell down the shaft that he had heard and would summon help, and then went off at top speed to contact a rescue-party.

It arrived, as rescue-parties do, in an astonishingly short time: experts with ropes and tackle, led by a man who knew Gaping Ghyll as well as any man alive. They descended the shaft and, led by the shouts of the marooned men, worked their way by a devious but possible route to the mass of rock on to which the party were perilously and desperately clinging—literally for dear life. For by now, though the rate of rise had slowed down, the water was already lapping at the ledge on which they were perched. Already it had begun to wash over the smooth rock, making it harder than ever to hold on to.

The rescue-party had laddering as well as ropes: tackle that made it possible to escape from the rock wall without climbing down into the swirling black water. But by the time the laddering had been fixed and the last man had clambered on to it, the water had risen so far that it demanded a great muscular effort even to remain on the rock: the rescue-party had arrived with no more than seconds to spare. If it had not been for that chance fell-walker it would not have arrived at all.

Much of Gaping Ghyll—perhaps most of it—has now been probed and plumbed, surveyed and charted; but all the experts who descend it when conditions permit are agreed in believing that its final mysteries have yet to be laid bare. That Yorkshire pot-hole, which threw out a challenge to John Birkbeck and later to Edouard-Alfred Martel, still holds out that challenge. Only in small fragments will it yield up its innate mysteries. But while the challenge lasts, there will always be men to take it up: men who are carrying on the great tradition of pot-holing, who are happiest and most fulfilled in their work when that work takes them in search of the unknown, the difficult, the hazardous in that wilderness of passage, tunnel, crawl, squeeze, shaft and cavern carved by Nature deep down below the surface of the earth.

BIBLIOGRAPHY

There are many books about speleology and pot-holing, and they are being added to every year. Among them are the following:

BAKER, E. A.: *Caving*
BAUMANN, HANS: *Caves of the Great Hunters*
CADOUX, JEAN: *One Thousand Metres Down*
CASTERET, NORBERT: *Cave Men New and Old*
CASTERET, NORBERT: *Darkness Under the Earth*
CASTERET, NORBERT: *Descent of Pierre Saint-Martin*
CASTERET, NORBERT: *My Caves*
CASTERET, NORBERT: *Ten Years Under the Earth*
CULLINGFORD, G. H. D.: *British Caving*
CULLINGFORD, G. H. D.: *Exploring Caves*
DANIEL, GLYN: *Lascaux and Carnac*
DOUGLAS, J. S.: *Caves of Mystery*
FRANKE, HERBERT: *Wilderness Under the Earth*
LAVOUR, GUY DE: *Caves and Cave Diving*
LÜBKE, ANTON: *The World of Caves*
TAZIEFF, HAROUN: *Caves of Adventure*
THORNBER (and others): *Britain Underground*

INDEX

149